Story w[riting]

PHILIP BOWDITCH

Teacher Timesavers

Published by Scholastic Ltd,
Villiers House,
Clarendon Avenue,
Leamington Spa,
Warwickshire CV32 5PR

© 1997 Scholastic Ltd

234567890   890123456

Author Philip Bowditch
Editor Clare Gallaher
Sub editor Kate Pearce
Series designer Joy White
Designers Toby Long and Micky Pledge
Illustrations Roger Fereday/Linda Rogers Associates
Cover illustration Frances Lloyd
Cover photograph Martyn Chillmaid

Designed using Aldus Pagemaker

British Library Cataloguing-in-Publication Data
A catalogue record for this book is
available from the British Library.

ISBN 0-590-53457-2

All rights reserved. This book is sold subject to the condition that it shall not, by way of trade or otherwise, be lent, hired out or otherwise circulated without the publisher's prior consent in any form of binding or cover other than that in which it is published and without a similar condition, including this condition, being imposed upon the subsequent purchaser.

No part of this publication may be reproduced, stored in a retrieval system, or transmitted, in any form or by any means, electronic, mechanical, photocopying, recording or otherwise, without the prior permission of the publisher. This book remains copyright, although permission is granted to copy pages 15 to 144 for classroom distribution and use only in the school which has purchased the book, or by the teacher who has purchased this book and in accordance with the CLA licensing agreement. Photocopying permission is given for purchasers only and not for borrowers of books from any lending service.

Contents

Teachers' notes — 5

All about stories
Different story types — 15
Different stories chart — 16
Reading story openings — 17
Planning story openings — 18
Ways to start stories — 19
Writing story openings — 20
Describing the seaside — 21
Describing different characters — 22
Describing a prince — 23
Good and bad characters — 24
Events in stories — 25
Chain of events — 26
Ways to end stories — 27
Writing story endings — 28

Scary stories
Scary similes: 1 — 29
Scary similes: 2 — 30
Scary alliteration — 31
Scary story ingredients — 32
My monster — 33
My monster story — 34

Animal stories
Safari animals — 35
Safari story — 36
Animal opposites — 37
Creature feature — 38
Reading an animal story — 39
Writing an animal story — 40
Animal tales — 41
The chase — 42

Crime stories
Wanted poster — 43
Crime by numbers — 44
Reporter's notebook — 45
Burglary interview — 46
Headline news — 47

Sports stories
Football fun — 48
Actions in sport — 49
Characters in sport — 50
Problems in sport — 51
Ordering chapter headings — 52
Writing chapter headings — 53
Sport story — 54
Sports commentators — 55
The competition — 56

Adventure stories
John's journey — 57
Jungle adventure — 58
Characters in adventure stories — 59
Adventure story chart — 60
Story ingredients — 61
Exploration adventure — 62

Fairy stories
Fairy stories list — 63
Writing fairy story openings — 64
Jack and the Beanstalk — 65
Little Red Riding Hood — 66
Making fairy stories modern: 1 — 67
Making fairy stories modern: 2 — 68
Leon and the Sad Giant — 69
Different endings — 70

Real-life stories
How I felt — 71
This is my life — 72
Feelings can change — 73
Friendship story — 74
Friends and enemies — 75
Which person? — 76

New situations 77

Space stories
Space journey 78
My pen-pal's an alien! 79
Alien visitor 80
Astronaut file 81
Blast off! 82
On the planet 83
The message 84
Planet in danger story 85

School stories
In the morning 86
School record files 87
Problems in school 88
A teacher's day 89
Finding out about school 90

Festival and celebration stories
Celebration stories 91
Festivals and events 92
Santa's midnight journey 93
Describing festivals 94
Festival titles 95
Party story 96

Historical stories
May's photographs 97
Albert's story 98
Time-travellers in Ancient Greece 99
Spanish Armada report 100
Railway journey 101
World War II diary 102
Time capsule 103
Historical settings 104

Mixed bag of stories
Weather story 105
Weather myth 106
Secret places 107
Fire! 108
Holiday postcard 109
Into the future 110
Western story 111
Science story 112
Shipwreck 113
Musical story 114
Aircraft story 115
The incredible present 116
Changing places 117
Pollution 118
How do they feel? 119
Competition story 120
Cautionary tales 121
Disaster! 122
Story titles: 1 123
Story titles: 2 124

Redrafting and language skills
Redrafting your story 125
Choosing the best words 126
The language of story writing 127
Writing in sentences 128
Bag of nouns 129
All sorts of nouns 130
Adjectives 131
Verbs 132
Adverbs 133
Conjunctions 134
Paragraphs 135
Direct speech 136
Story tenses 137

Pro formas
Planning your story 138
Writing story openings 139
Describing the character 140
Describing the setting 141
Storyboard 142
Problems and solutions 143
Writing story endings 144

Teacher Timesavers: Story writing

About the author
Philip Bowditch is currently a Deputy Head in a large junior school. He has co-ordinated English in primary schools and taught English across secondary, middle and primary sectors.

Introduction
Teaching children to write stories is a vital element of the programmes of study for English in the primary curriculum. The activities in this book offer imaginative enjoyable ways to encourage children from five to eleven years of age to create, explore and analyse stories. Many children have enormous enthusiasm for writing stories. Sometimes, however, they need support, structure and guidance on how to organise their ideas. These activities provide a framework on which to build children's skills, knowledge and confidence as story writers.

The first chapter, 'All about stories', helps children to explore particular aspects of story writing, including describing settings, identifying story genres, experimenting with different ways to end stories, and so on.

In the following chapters children are given opportunities to write stories across a wide range of genres, from adventure, crime and real-life stories to fairy stories. Each chapter is identified by a pictorial genre symbol which appears on each sheet. Activities offer children exciting and challenging ways to explore the conventions of each genre (for example, characters, settings, events) and encourage children to write in a range of forms such as letters, newspaper reports and diaries, using both first- and third-person narrative. They are also given opportunities to write for clearly defined audiences, including younger children and their peers.

The penultimate chapter, 'Redrafting and language skills', focuses on the writing process. The activities give children the opportunity to develop greater understanding and control of the language they use and to evaluate and redraft their stories.

The final chapter, 'Pro formas', provides a range of generic story-planning sheets. These activities, along with those in 'All about stories' and 'Redrafting and language skills', can be used to build story-writing skills and to provide support for activities in other chapters.

Teachers' notes suggest practical ways to make each activity dynamic, interactive, challenging and enjoyable for children through paired, group, individual and whole-class work. They also suggest how resources, including stories, poems and video-clips, and children's own experiences can be used to provide further stimulus and discussion points for children's story writing.

Suggestions for support and extension activities are made where appropriate. Various strategies for differentiation are used, including breaking the activity down into smaller steps, offering suggestions for resources which could be used to further support or to extend children, explaining how the task may be done at a more advanced or simpler level and suggesting further activities.

❍ denotes suggestions for support activities.
❑ denotes suggestions for extension activities.

All about stories
Different story types Show the children some book covers and read them brief extracts from stories. Ask them to identify the type of stories or genre in which these stories can be categorised, encouraging them to identify ingredients from

Teachers' Notes

each story and to look at the pictures on the book covers to give them clues about the different story types.
❑ Challenge children to identify authors and titles for each story type.

Different stories chart Discuss a genre which the children know well, identifying typical places, characters and events in stories from that genre.
❍ Ask children to select a story book that they have read, and identify the characters, places and events in the book.
❑ Ask children to write a review of a particular genre, listing titles they have read, comparing characters, places and events.

Reading story openings Read aloud story openings and ask children to identify each story's genre.
❑ Suggest that the children write the next sentence in each story.

Planning story openings Encourage children to look at the information in the pictures and to use their imagination for the characters' names and the places.
❑ Cut out a series of up-to-date pictures from newspapers and magazines. Ask the children to look at the pictures and list ideas for a story opening – characters, a setting and an event – discussing and comparing their ideas.

Ways to start stories Explain the four ways to start a story. Read an example of a story opening aloud and ask children to identify the type of opening.
❑ Let the children work with story books, reading them and then identifying the way each story starts. Discuss with them which openings they liked most and why.

Teacher Timesavers: Story writing

Writing story openings Show children a picture of your choice and ask them in pairs or groups to write a story opening fulfilling one of the categories. Listen to the different examples and compare them.
❏ Ask children to select one picture and write four different openings for it.

Describing the seaside Help stimulate ideas by reading a poem or a piece of descriptive prose, or by showing a video extract about the seaside. Brainstorm ideas for one aspect of the task, for example sounds at the seaside, before you give children the sheet. Encourage them to compare their lists when they have finished them.
❍ Give children a list of words which they can select for the appropriate box, encouraging them to include their own.
❏ Ask children to write a description of a setting of their choice.

Describing different characters Collect a series of pictures of different people to show to the children. Ask them to identify what each person is doing, how they feel and how they look.

Describing a prince Read aloud a character description from a story book. Ask the children to remember all of the words the writer uses to describe how the character looks. Explain that writers paint pictures with describing words or adjectives. Ask the children to identify adjectives to describe objects around them.
❏ Children should be able to complete each of the boxes without the use of the vocabulary box. They can then go on to compile adjective lists for other characters, for example witches or cowboys/cowgirls.

Good and bad characters Discuss the fact that many stories have contrasting characters such as good characters and bad characters, for example Snow White and the wicked queen. Ask the children to describe the personalities of opposing characters in stories which they know.
❍ Give children specific characters to describe.
❏ Let the children use words of their own to complete the lists. Then, using story books, ask them to find descriptions of good and bad characters.

Events in stories Describe the first picture on the sheet. Ask the children to identify as many ideas as they can for what could happen next.
❏ Ask children to write an alternative next event for each of the pictures.

Chain of events Explain to the children that many stories are based around a series of related events. Choose a story which all the children know. Ask them to list the four main events in the story.
❍ Give children a list of options from which they can sequence events correctly.
❏ Ask children to choose one story opening idea and list as many different chains of events as they can for it.

Ways to end stories Explain the different types of endings, then ask children to identify how stories which you read to them end. Discuss which type of ending children like most and why.
❏ Suggest that the children read the endings of a range of stories and identify the category which is appropriate for each one.

Writing story endings Discuss where each picture is set, what is happening, who the main character is and so on before the children write their story endings.
❏ Let the children try to write each type of ending for each picture.

Scary stories

Scary similes: 1 Hold up a brightly coloured object and ask the children to complete a phrase to describe the object, for example 'red like...' Explain that writers often compare one thing with another to enable us to create pictures in our mind.
❏ Ask children, working in pairs, to list alternative ideas for each simile. Discuss which similes work best and why.

Scary similes: 2 Read aloud the first sentence from the story and ask the children to list words which would complete the simile. Allow discussion time in pairs or groups before they complete the sheet. Discuss the similes, and the images or pictures evoked by them.
❏ Let the children tell a story which uses similes by playing 'The scary story game'. Explain that one child will start to tell a scary story. When he or she reaches the first part of a simile, the telling of the story passes to the child on the right. For example, 'When Duncan woke up he realised it was as cold as...' The similes generated by 'The scary story game' can be made into a class book and used as a reference when children are writing their own stories.

Scary alliteration Recite a saying such as 'Peter Piper picked a peck of pickled pepper.' Ask the children what they noticed about the saying. Explain what alliteration is. Give groups an object, for example a ball, and ask them to devise a sentence with as many alliterations as they can, starting with the same letter as the object. Discuss the effects created by the use of alliteration in writing.
❏ Ask children to write alliterative sentences or phrases to describe a scary character.

Scary story ingredients Stimulate children's imagination by reading extracts from scary stories to them. For each story, ask them to identify the place in which the story takes place, describe the weather and recall objects which

were included in the story. Children could read extracts from their favourite scary stories to the whole class.
○ Talk to children about scary stories which they have read, seen or heard. Encourage them to identify scary ingredients in these stories and incorporate them in their lists.
❏ Ask the children to devise their own categories and make their own lists of ingredients before writing their stories, using the headings on the sheet as prompts for ideas.

My monster Discuss monsters which the children have read about in stories, or seen in films. Include points such as how the monsters behaved, and what they looked like, in the discussion.
○ Give the children pictures of monsters from story books to help them generate ideas.
❏ Let the children use the sheet as a planning sheet before writing a description of their monster.

My monster story Draw children's attention to the 'To think about' section on the sheet. Allow discussion time on this before writing begins. Remind the children to include the description of the monster in their story if they completed the previous activity.
○ Let children read their choice of story opening on tape and continue their story orally.
❏ Encourage the children to re-read their stories and consider how they could improve the characterisation of their monster. Do they need to add more information about its appearance, for example, and how can they achieve this?

Animal stories

Safari animals Show the children a picture (in a picture book or cut out from a magazine or newspaper) of one of the animals on the sheet. Brainstorm words which they could use to describe the animal.
○ Give children pictures of all four animals to which they can refer.
❏ Ask children to write a description of each animal, using sentences.

Safari story Show the children a picture of an animal before distributing the sheets. Ask them to give an oral description of the animal and explain what it is doing.
○ With children working in pairs, give each pair names of different animals written on pieces of card or drawings/pictures of animals. Ask one child to read the name of the animal and the other to identify a word to describe it.
❏ Ask children to write a description of the scene depicted on the sheet.

Animal opposites Tell the children a story of two 'opposite animals' who make friends and help each other; an example is the story about the lion who had a thorn in his paw being helped by the mouse, who pulled it out.
○ Give a group of children an example of two different animals. Ask them to list ideas for how one animal might help the other.

Creature feature Ask children to identify their favourite animal. Discuss where the animal lives, what it looks like, what it eats, and what its babies are called.
❏ Give children further categories in which to list information on each creature, or ask them to devise their own, for example man's attitude towards the creature, and how the creature catches its food.

Reading an animal story Ask the children to describe the different things that their pets do each day. Where do they sleep? What do they eat? Do they follow the same routine every day?
○ Pair more able readers with less able ones.
❏ Ask children to plan a sequence of events for Kevin's next day. Discuss their suggestions and compare them.

Writing an animal story Video extracts from children's animal cartoons or animal short stories provide excellent stimuli for this activity.
○ Write some sentence starters for the children which they can use as a guide to draw upon, if required (for example, In the morning... In the afternoon... In the evening...).
❏ Encourage children to show the animal's thoughts and feelings in their story. Ask them to suggest different ways in which this could be achieved, stating which ways they think would work best and why.

Animal tales Read the children a traditional story such as 'How the leopard got its spots'. Allocate an animal to each group of children and ask them to devise orally a story outline for concepts such as why the ant is so small, or how the giraffe got a long neck.
○ Give children a list of animals. Ask them to write a feature about each animal which an animal tale could explain, for example a heron could have an animal tale about its beak.
❏ Ask children to think of possible storylines for each animal. Discuss their ideas and ask them which storyline they think would make the most entertaining story, and why.

The chase Working in groups, or as a whole class, brainstorm all of the animals which are chased by humans. Encourage the children to give reasons for the pursuit of the animals – perhaps for sport, for example, or for food.
❏ Ask children to make a corresponding list for the sounds, smells and feelings which the *humans* will encounter. Emphasise that the children should produce a story which has parallel storylines, switching from a description

of the animal, and what is happening to it, to the humans and vice versa.

Crime stories

Wanted poster Brainstorm different types of crime with the children. Explain the term 'alias' if necessary.
◯ Fill in a Wanted poster which the children can refer to as an exemplar.
❏ Let children design their own Wanted poster and devise categories in which details about the criminal can be placed.

Crime by numbers With groups or the whole class, brainstorm possible objects, characters and crimes which could be incorporated in crime stories, as well as appropriate settings.

Reporter's notebook Ask children whether they or anyone they know has ever been a victim of crime. Discuss the type of information which a newspaper reporter would need to find out about a crime if he or she were researching for a newspaper report.
◯ The prompt questions at the side of the notebook provide a framework for a report. Ask children to answer them, writing in sentences.

Burglary interview Ask children to imagine that a burglar broke into the school the previous evening. Read out the first question and encourage children to devise as wide a range of oral responses as possible.
◯ Let children work in pairs. Ask one child in each pair to read the questions and the other child to answer them orally. Record the interviews on tape.
❏ Encourage children to write their own questions to ask the victim.

Headline news Show the children a range of newspaper headlines. Ask them what they think each headline is about. Discuss roughly how many words each headline has and whether the story behind the report is always clear from the headline.
◯ Give children examples of headlines to choose from for the first activity. Ask children to list ideas for a setting, characters and events which would be appropriate for each headline.
❏ Analyse different types of newspaper headlines with the children, for example factual, sensational or colloquial. Draw their attention to alliterative headlines and see if they can devise their own.

Sports stories

Football fun Let the children watch a video-clip from a football match. Ask them to think of events that can happen at a football match and make a list, working in groups.
❏ Ask children to number the pictures, and then devise as many different sequences as they can for them. For example, the story could start with a team winning the cup at the end of the season.

Actions in sport Show children various extracts from sports events on video. Ask children to say where each event is taking place and list words to describe each character's movements.
◯ Give children a list of verbs to help them to complete the first part of each sentence.
❏ Ask children to list two or more verbs for each example. Discuss with them which verb they think works best and why.

Characters in sport Ask children to identify different sportsmen and women. For each one discuss his or her body type, skills and mental attitude. Discuss which skills are needed to play different sports successfully.
◯ Provide the children with pictures of well-known sporting personalities. Ask the children to list words which could describe each person.
❏ Let the children choose a sporting personality and write a monologue which reveals the person's thoughts before, during and after a race or match.

Problems in sport Give groups of children a card which has a sport written on it. Ask each group to brainstorm ideas for things that can go wrong for competitors in that sport.
◯ Discuss where each sport is set and what happens at each sporting event before asking the children to think of problems.

Ordering chapter headings Read some chapter headings from story books to the children and ask them to predict what could happen in each chapter.
◯ Cut out the chapter headings on the sheet beforehand so that children can experiment with different orders before they write down their answers.
❏ Ask children to write the opening and closing paragraph of each chapter.

Writing chapter headings Go through the first two parts of the story outline and ask children for suggestions for chapter headings.
◯ Give children written suggestions for each chapter and then ask them to order them appropriately.
❏ Encourage the children to use figures of speech such as alliteration, similes and onomatopoeia in their headings.

Sport story Ask children to choose a sport which they would like to write a story about. Explain that they can choose whether to write a story about a sporting competition, one individual player/athlete or about a sport supporter.
◯ Tell children to list the events in their story on a separate sheet of paper, and then highlight the events which will go in each chapter. They

should complete the chapter headings last.
❏ Ask children to devise a chain of events for their story first.

Sports commentators Play children a tape of a sports commentary. Ask them to recall the events the commentator has just described. Give each group of children a sport. Ask them to list typical words, phrases or sentences that a sports commentator might use for the sport. Compare their ideas.
❍ Give children the lists which groups made in your introduction to the activity.
❏ Let children record their own sports commentary on to tape. Encourage them to emulate the style of a sports commentator. Then listen to the commentary with the children and ask them what happens to the pitch and volume of the commentator's voice during the event.

The competition Show children clips from videos of different sports. Ask them to identify as many competitions as they can for each sport, for example the FA Cup, the European Cup and so on if the sport is football.
❍ Provide children with a picture of a sporting personality participating in the sport which they have chosen to help them to generate ideas.
❏ Ask children to compile a list of sports terminology for their chosen sport, ensuring that they have explained the meaning of each word and the context in which it is used. Make these lists available for all children to refer to during their story writing.

Adventure stories

John's journey Ask the children to explain orally what is happening in each picture, and to describe the setting and the weather.
❍ Write sentences which explain the remaining three pictures for children to match correctly.

❏ Ask children to imagine what happened to John when he reached hospital and to write it as a story.

Jungle adventure Before children look at the picture on the sheet, ask them to describe the weather, wildlife, places and plant life in a jungle region. Ask them to imagine what they would see, hear, smell and feel if they were standing in the middle of a jungle.
❍ Discuss the detail in the illustration with the children. Ask them which categories each object or living thing could fit into. For example, could Kate have seen, heard and smelled animals?
❏ Ask children to write a description of the jungle, using sentences.

Characters in adventure stories Ask groups to list as many adventure story heroes/heroines and villains as they can from adventure stories that they know. (Although there are many different kinds of adventure story, these 'Adventure stories' sheets cover the popular sort, such as *Indiana Jones* or *Superman*, with which the children will be most familiar.)
❍ Ask children to explain what each word in the 'ideas' list means before they decide which character type it would best describe.
❏ Let children analyse the behaviour and personalities of two different adventure story heroes/heroines or villains. Discuss which character they think makes the best hero/villain and why.

Adventure story chart Watch the opening sequence of an adventure video, or read the opening of an adventure story. Ask children to identify the relevant ingredients on the chart.
❍ Read extracts from an adventure story to the children. Give them a selection of ingredients from the chart with which to identify the corresponding components in the story.

❏ Ask children to list the ingredients of two adventure stories and then compare the two stories, focusing on aspects of the stories that they liked or disliked, explaining why.

Story ingredients Discuss how a story from a book or film would fit into this plan. Provide time for children to discuss their ideas for their story.

Exploration adventure Watch extracts from a video such as *Labyrinth* which shows the main character encountering a range of problems during her adventure. Ask children to recall what the problems were and how the main character overcame them.
❏ Challenge children to devise more than one solution to each problem. Discuss which solution they think is best and why.

Fairy stories

Fairy stories list Show the opening sequence of fairy story videos, for example *Aladdin*. Ask children to identify the good and bad characters and where the stories are set.
❍ Have a range of simple fairy story books available so that children can use these for ideas.

Writing fairy story openings Suggest to the children that fairy stories can have different kinds of openings. Read extracts from fairy stories which begin in different ways: by describing the good character; by showing a conversation between the good and the bad character; or by describing the setting. Alternatively, devise your own story openings.
❏ Ask children to read their openings to each other and discuss which ones they think would make the reader want to continue reading, and why.

Jack and the Beanstalk Before they look at the sheet, ask children to identify the main

characters in *Jack and the Beanstalk* and the setting of the story.
❍ Give children phrases which they can match with the correct sentences to complete them.
❏ Ask children to make a list of or draw four more pictures which could be added to the story at any point to make the story more detailed, for example a drawing of the goose which laid the golden egg.

Little Red Riding Hood Before they see the sheet, ask children to list orally the events, characters and setting in *Little Red Riding Hood*.
❍ Suggest that the children work in pairs and perform a role-play, with one child speaking as the wolf, the other as Little Red Riding Hood.

Making fairy stories modern: 1 Before beginning the activity, discuss the idea of making traditional story ingredients modern. Give groups or pairs one ingredient from a fairy story and ask them to devise ideas for modern equivalents. Compare different suggestions.
❍ Give children a selection of 'old' ingredients from which to choose.
❏ Rather than using the sheet, ask the children to make their own list of ingredients from *Cinderella* and think of modern equivalents.

Making fairy stories modern: 2 Discuss the conventions of traditional fairy stories, for example starting with 'Once upon a time', or presenting a happy ending. Ask the children for suggestions about how these could be changed to make them 'modern'.
❏ Encourage children to change as many aspects of the story as they can. Discuss how direct speech could be made more contemporary.

Leon and the Sad Giant Look at and discuss the pictures with the children. Ask them to describe Leon and the giant – what they look like, how they are feeling and what they are doing in each picture. Draw children's attention to the castle in the background and ask how it could relate to the conversation between Leon and the giant.
❍ Let the children work in pairs, first orally with one child speaking as the giant, the other as Leon. Write speech marks on the sheet to help the children with the second question.

Different endings Read children the ending of a fairy story. Ask them in groups to devise alternative endings which are different from the original (these may be happy, sad or neutral).
❍ Write down how *Goldilocks* and *Sleeping Beauty* end, then ask children to offer ideas for different endings.
❏ Ask children to write two different endings for the fairy story they choose, one of which is happy and the other sad. Discuss whether any fairy stories have sad endings, and why.

Real-life stories

How I felt Ask different children to complete the sentences, 'I felt happy when...' orally. Point out to the children that different events make each of us feel a different way.
❍ As an alternative to writing a full story, ask the children to complete the sentences on the sheet using the name of their character at the beginning of each sentence. For example, 'Jess felt happy when her mum said she could choose a pet for her birthday.'

This is my life Discuss happy, sad, embarrassing and scary events which the children have experienced. Ask children to tell the rest of the class in detail about their experiences and draw their attention to the different types of information they include, for example how old they were, where it happened and so on.
❍ Let the children describe their chosen experiences on tape, having planned their ideas on the sheet.
❏ Ask children to add a paragraph to their story explaining how they feel looking back on the event. Have their feelings changed in any way?

Feelings can change Brainstorm all of the different feelings a character might experience having found that he or she is going to have a brother or sister. Draw on children's own experiences.
❏ Ask children to list alternative feelings for each character.

Friendship story Ask children to identify which qualities they value in a friend and why.
❍ Ask children to work with a friend to prepare an oral presentation to the class or a group about their friendship, using the prompts on the sheet to help them.

Friends and enemies Show children how to plan their story from a title by illustrating with one title on the board or OHP.
❍ Discuss ideas for characters, settings and events with children for each story title before they brainstorm ideas for their story.

Which person? Read aloud extracts from stories written in the first and the third person. Ask the children how the two styles of writing are different.
❍ Underline the words in the story openings which categorise them as first or third person.
❏ Ask children which style of writing they would use to write different stories. Ask them to justify the choices they have made.

New situations Explain to the children that the audience for this story is a group of young children and that these stories will be read to them. How do they think the younger children would feel about their first visit to the dentist, for example? Why would they have this response? Look at examples of texts written for young children, analysing the range of language used and the format of the books.

Space stories

Space journey Draw children's attention to the appearance of the characters and what they are wearing. Discuss what is happening in each picture with the children to give them a sense of the structure of the story before they write in the speech bubbles and continue the story.
❍ Let children work in pairs and role-play what the characters are saying.

My pen-pal's an alien! Discuss with the children what questions they would ask an alien from outer space about itself and its life.
❍ For the second part of the activity, ask children to work in pairs, with one person speaking as the human and the other as the alien.
❏ Ask the children to write a story which describes the events that led up to the message appearing on the computer screen and explains what happened as a result of the message.

Alien visitor Ask children who the characters are, what the relationship between them is and where each picture is set.
❍ Use the storyboard on page 142 in place of the second activity on the sheet, asking children to draw and/or write about one alien's visit.

Astronaut file Show children pictures of astronauts. Discuss the kind of skills and personality an astronaut would need.
❍ Give children posters or pictures on which to base their file.
❏ Suggest that the children use the format of the file to give them ideas for their own astronaut-file application form, with a wider range of categories and questions.

Blast off! Show children a video of a rocket or shuttle launch. Let them brainstorm, in groups or as a class, the sounds and events which occur as a rocket is launched.

On the planet Outline some events which children could include in their story. Explain that they should write the story as if they are the astronaut. Read the starter lines to illustrate how to write in the first person.

The message Check that the children understand how to use the decoder by writing words on the board for them to translate.
❍ Translate the first word for the children, before giving them the sheet, to provide them with a model.

Planet in danger story Ask children to identify problems people face on planet Earth and how these problems might be solved. Explain that they can use similar problems in their story.

School stories

In the morning Ask the children who they see in the morning when they arrive at school, what each person is usually doing and where.
❍ Cut the parts of each sentence out so that children can experiment to work out which parts of the sentence make sense together.

School record files Read the school record file with the children. Ask them to identify the facts about themselves which would go on the file. Emphasise the importance of being imaginative in their descriptions when filling in the details about their character.
❏ Ask the children to devise their own school record files, using the pro forma on the sheet to obtain ideas.

Problems in school Discuss the problems which children may encounter at school, and ways for how each one could be solved. Discuss how different types of problems could make characters feel. For example, do they feel angry or left out? Stress that each problem can be solved in a number of different ways.
❍ Give children a list which has some ideas for solutions to school problems.

A teacher's day Working in groups, let the children discuss ideas which would be appropriate for each box, before presenting their ideas to the rest of the class.
❏ Ask the children to include the teacher's thoughts and feelings in their story.

Finding out about school Discuss with the children how they felt on their first day at school or their first day at a new school, particularly aspects such as sounds and smells that they can remember.

Festival and celebration stories

Celebration stories Explain to the children there is not necessarily a right and wrong order for each story but that they should try to find the order which they think works best.

Festivals and events Ask children to identify their favourite festival. Discuss what happens during each festival.

Santa's midnight journey Read the first example aloud. Ask the children to work in pairs to find as many alternatives as they can. Before children start to write their own description, read extracts from *The Night Before Christmas* by Clement Moore (North South Books).
❏ Ask children to read each other's stories and identify the verbs that they have used.

Describing festivals Ask children to bring in objects which are related to a festival, such as decorations, clothes, cards and so on. Let the children show the items that they have brought in to the rest of the class. Discuss with the

Teacher Timesavers: Story writing

children the smells, sounds, colours and feelings they associate with their festival.
Festival titles Show the children one title from the sheet. Give them time in groups to decide which festival the story could be about and to brainstorm ideas for possible characters and settings. Compare each group's ideas.
❍ Provide children with a list of possible festivals from which to choose.
❑ Let the children devise other story titles for each festival that they have listed.
Party story Discuss with the children the events which have happened at parties they have been to: games they played, the best moments, worst moments and so on.
❍ Show the children some completed party invitations so that they can use these as a reference point for their own invitations.

Historical stories

The following notes apply to all of the activities in this chapter. The first two activities have been designed for children whose abilities are within Key Stage 1/Scottish levels A–B. The next four sheets build children's story-writing skills through topics from the Key Stage 2/Scottish levels C–E history programme of study. The last two sheets are generic and can be used for either stage.

Introduce each activity by providing children with a range of source material relevant to the topic they are studying, for example photographs from your own album for 'May's photographs' or pictures of various historical settings for the 'Historical settings' sheet. Encourage children to think about how they would feel if they were living in that particular historical period. What has been the effect of changes that have been made between how things were then and how they are now? Have these differences been for the better or have things been made worse? Ask children to justify their answers.
❍ Children may need to discuss the planning aspects of these sheets in groups before they start to write. Again, source material, especially pictures, will remind children of the historical information they know and stimulate their imagination.

Mixed bag of stories

Weather story Read out each of the descriptive words on the sheet and ask children to identify what type of weather they would apply to.
Weather myth Explain the definition of a myth to the children. If possible, read a myth that explains some natural phenomena. Give each group of children one type of weather on the sheet and ask them to devise a myth to explain it, orally. Listen to the ideas from each group and compare them.
❍ Suggest that children use their group's myth as the starting point for their story.
❑ In pairs or small groups, let children read their stories aloud to the class, with the addition of appropriate sound effects.
Secret places Read an extract from a book which describes a character finding a secret place, for example *The Secret Garden* by Frances Hodgson Burnett (Puffin). Ask the children to identify other secret places that they have read about or seen characters discovering. Discuss possible reasons for places being kept secret.
Fire! Discuss who the characters might be and where the story is set.
Holiday postcard Ask children about holidays that they have had. What did they do? Who went with them? What did they enjoy most and least?
❍ Give children completed postcards to use as models for their writing and to show them the address format.
Into the future Ask children to discuss in groups how far into the future they would go if they were able to travel there for a short time. Ask them to justify the choices they have made.
❍ Before children plan their ideas, discuss how things like school, food and clothes, for example, might change in the future.
Western story Read an extract from a typical Western story, or watch extracts from a Western television series or film. Ask children to brainstorm all of the ingredients in traditional Western stories.
❑ Explain that traditional Western stories often show men as macho heroes and women as weak victims, but some current Western films have reversed this. Ask children to write a Western story which reverses traditional trends.
Science story Before giving children the sheet, read aloud the ingredients in the bottles. Ask children to categorise them as settings, characters or events.
Shipwreck Set the scene for the children before they start writing. Ask them to imagine that they are walking along a high cliff, with the sea crashing on the rocks below them. Explain that they are going to describe a shipwreck taking place, and that they should try to make the reader feel as if he or she is there too.
❑ Explain the term 'onomatopoeia' to children. Encourage them to use it in their descriptions.
Musical story Show children a variety of classical musical instruments. Ask them to predict whether each one plays loudly or softly, or plays high or low notes. To which family of instruments does each one belong?
❑ Suggest that the children write the story from

the point of view of the instrument. Discuss whether the story will work most successfully in the first or third person and why.

Aircraft story Draw children's attention to the aircraft language in the box on the sheet. Outline briefly how a plane is controlled and explain that the airport control tower will give the pilot of a plane instructions about how to land the aircraft. Encourage the children to empathise with the passenger's feelings and thoughts when finding that he or she is in charge of the plane. Explain how to write dialogue.

The incredible present Discuss the subject of present-giving with the children. Ask what the presents were, who they gave them to and why they enjoyed giving them.
❍ Put a gift-wrapped box on the table and ask the children to imagine what is in it. Use this as a starting point for the story.
❏ Ask children to identify someone they would like to give a present to, what it would be and why they would choose that particular present.

Changing places Discuss with the children what they think their parents, or relatives they know well, do each day. Ask them to imagine how these people feel about the things they have to do. What would they enjoy doing? Is there anything that they would dread having to do?
❍ Give children a framework of sentences to complete (for example, In the morning... After I had eaten I...).
❏ Discuss who they would most like to change places with and why.

Pollution Ask children to identify which types of pollution make them angry, and ask them to explain why.
❍ Ask children to discuss the causes and effects of different types of pollution, orally in groups, before they fill in the chart.

❏ Give pairs or a group of children a card which has a type of pollution written on it. Ask them to brainstorm as many adjectives as they can for the type of pollution (for example, 'greasy' and 'slimy' for oil pollution). Ask them to add adjectives to their story.

How do they feel? Ask children to identify the setting, character and event in each picture.
❏ Ask children to write down what they think will happen to the character next in each picture.

Competition story Brainstorm with children the different competitions that they know. These may be television shows that they have watched, or competitions in which they or their parents have taken part.
❍ Let the children work in pairs or small groups to explain to each other the rules and stages of the competition that they have chosen before they plan their ideas.
❏ Ask children to read their finished story to a friend who should offer advice about how the tension and excitement of the story could be increased.

Cautionary tales Tell the children a cautionary tale, such as *The Boy Who Cried Wolf*. Ask them to identify how the character behaved and what the consequences of his behaviour were.
❍ Let children work in small groups to generate ideas for possible bad behaviour or actions and what the consequences of each one could be.
❏ Suggest that the children choose one of their ideas and write a cautionary tale.

Disaster! Ask children to list as many environmental disasters as they can. Either as a class or in groups, discuss possible settings for each disaster and the effects it would have on the settings.
❍ Give children pictures depicting each disaster, which they can use as a base for their ideas.

❏ Ask children whether there are ever any beneficial consequences as a result of environmental disasters. Encourage them to show both good and bad effects in their stories.

Story titles: 1 Give pairs or groups a story title (you may wish to cut the titles up and put them into a bag which the children can use as a lucky dip) and ask them to brainstorm characters, places and events. Discuss the ideas from different groups.
❍ Help the children to brainstorm possible characters, settings and events for their story title before they start to write.
❏ Ask children to suggest an appropriate genre for each story title.

Story titles: 2 Discuss each picture with the class. Ask children to identify the setting, character(s), event and genre.
❏ Ask children to look at examples of story titles from books in the classroom. Ask them to try to identify what makes a good story title.

Redrafting and language skills

Redrafting your story Children can use this sheet to check their own work or each other's. You may wish to choose different areas to focus on redrafting and use this as a general prompt sheet.

Choosing the best words Read out the first sentence to be completed on the sheet. Ask the children to write down the word they would have used to complete the sentence. Listen to the range of options children devise. Explain to children that there are often many words of similar meaning which they can choose from in their story writing, and that it is up to them to decide which will have the effect they require.

The language of story writing Let children work in groups to identify information on story-book covers such as the author(s) and the title. Is it possible to glean any information about the setting, events, plot or characters from the cover?

Writing in sentences Read the opening two sentences of a story to the children, without pausing for the full stop. Ask them to identify where the full stop should have been.
❍ Let the children work in pairs, listening to each other read the passage to help them to decide where to place the full stops.

Bag of nouns and All sorts of nouns Review the definitions with the children before they start the tasks. Read examples to them from stories and ask them to categorise each one.

Adjectives Review the definition of an adjective with the children. Read them examples from story books of sentences which have adjectives. Ask them to identify the words that are adjectives.
❏ Ask children to write alliterative sentences describing each noun.

Verbs Review the definition of a verb with the children. Read extracts from story books and ask children to identify the verb(s) in each sentence.

Adverbs Review the definition of an adverb with the children. Give pairs or groups of children a verb and ask them to brainstorm adverbs for it. Listen to the different examples children offer.

Conjunctions Review the meaning of a conjunction and give the children some examples. Read two sentences and ask children to suggest a conjunction to join them.
❍ Give children a range of story books and ask them to compile a list of conjunctions.
❏ Give children a range of story books. Ask them to identify conjunctions, then list possible alternatives for each one. Discuss what purpose each conjunction serves by reading the sentence with each conjunction.

Paragraphs Explain when and why writers use paragraphs and how these are indicated (indent, extra line space). Let children identify paragraphs in books, newspapers and so on. Read an extract from a story and ask children to identify where the paragraph breaks should be.
❏ Ask children to read through a story, identifying where the paragraph breaks are, and whether each paragraph denotes a change in time, place or events.

Direct speech Review the rules of direct speech with the children. Read them an extract from a story which includes direct speech. When you read direct speech, change the tone or pitch of your voice. Ask children to identify where speech marks should start and finish.
❍ Fill in the indirect speech for the second task, so that children only have to write in the words characters actually say.
❏ Ask children to find examples of direct speech in story books. Ask them to make a list of rules about how punctuation is used before, during and after direct speech. Let the list be available for reference in the classroom.

Story tenses Review the difference between the past and present tense with the children. Give them examples of verbs in the past tense and ask them to change them to the present tense and vice versa.
❏ Ask children to read story openings and identify whether they are written in the past or present tense.

Pro formas

These sheets are generic to facilitate their use with any other sheets in the book. They provide a framework to help children to plan story ideas, write story openings, describe settings, plan events or write story endings.

The chart below identifies different aspects of story writing and lists page numbers where relevant activities for each aspect can be found. All these story-writing skills can be linked to requirements and guidelines for English in the UK national curricula.

Skills	Page Nos.
Genre	
✤analysing genre	15, 16, 17
✤devising story ingredients	32, 34, 40, 41, 42, 44, 56, 60, 61, 67, 68, 83, 90, 94, 96, 99, 101, 106, 110, 111, 112, 114, 120, 121, 138
Story openings	
✤analysing story openings	17, 19, 34, 76
✤writing story openings	18, 20, 38, 64, 111, 139
Setting	
✤describing the setting	21, 93, 104, 107, 122, 141
✤creating atmosphere	29, 30, 31, 105, 113
Characterisation	
✤general description	22, 33, 35, 36, 38, 43, 81, 87, 98, 140
✤describing personality, thoughts and feelings	24, 50, 59, 71, 73, 119
✤describing appearance	23, 35
✤relationships with others	37, 74, 75
Plot development	
✤predicting and describing events	25, 36, 49, 51, 58, 66, 69, 71, 72, 78, 80, 86, 92, 116
✤sequencing events	26, 39, 48, 57, 65, 89, 91, 97, 108, 142
✤problems and solutions	62, 84, 85, 88, 118, 143
Story endings	
✤analysing story endings	27, 70
✤writing story endings	28, 70, 144
Story titles	75, 95, 123, 124
Story chapters	52, 53, 54
Writing for different audiences	77, 103, 109
Writing in a range of styles	45, 46, 47, 55, 79, 100, 102, 109, 115, 117
Redrafting and language skills	125–137

Name _____

All about stories
Different story types

Different story types

✤ Match up each picture with the right story type.

Story types
horror
fairy
adventure
sport
animal
crime

✤ List as many other story types as you can on the back of this sheet.

Teacher Timesavers: Story writing

15

All about stories

Different stories chart

Different stories chart

✤ Fill in this chart with examples for each story type.

Story type	Characters	Places	Events	What you think of this type of story
animal stories	pigs	farmyard		
fairy stories	wicked queen	magic kingdom	spells	

✤ Choose another story type. Fill in the bottom row with examples from this.

Teacher Timesavers: Story writing

Name _____

All about stories
Reading story openings

Reading story openings

✣ Write a story type under each story opening.

| The lion crept silently through the jungle. | Prince Paul was reading his book of spells. | 'You are late for school again.' |

_____ _____ _____

| 'Goal!' yelled Alice. | Lightning flashed across the sky. | No one heard the robber smash the window. |

_____ _____ _____

Story types

fairy

horror

sport

animal

crime

school

Teacher Timesavers: Story writing 17

All about stories

Planning story openings

Name _____

Planning story openings

✤ For each picture make up the name of the character and place, then write down what is happening. Decide which story type each one is.

Character(s) _____

Place _____

Story type _____

Thing that is happening

Character(s) _____

Place _____

Story type _____

Thing that is happening

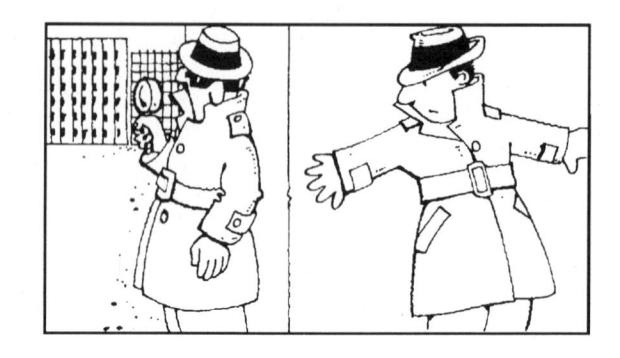

Character(s) _____

Place _____

Story type _____

Thing that is happening

Teacher Timesavers: Story writing

Name _____

All about stories
Ways to start stories

Ways to start stories

✤ Match each story opening with the way it starts.

Ways to start	• characters speaking	• describing the place
	• describing a character	• something happening

- The beach was smooth and sandy. Cool waves lapped lazily along the shore.

Way it starts _____

- The crowd stepped back as the engines roared. Fire burst forth as the rocket launched into space.

Way it starts _____

- 'It's not fair!' Lucy shouted.

Way it starts _____

- Steaming hay and pools of wet mud littered the old farmyard.

Way it starts _____

- She looked in despair at the mirror. Her long black hair and pale face were filthy.

Way it starts _____

- 'What's that?' Tim whispered. 'It's coming towards us!' replied Anna.

Way it starts _____

Teacher Timesavers: Story writing

All about stories

Writing story openings

Writing story openings

✤ Write a story opening for each of these pictures.
Try to write the opening using the way to start which is written beside each picture.

Describe the character.

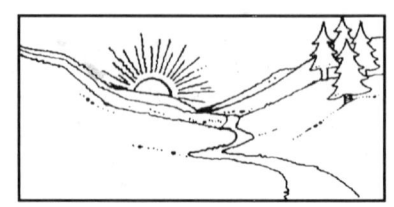

Describe the place.

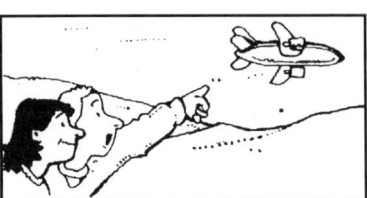

Describe what is happening.

Write what the characters are saying.

Teacher Timesavers: Story writing

Name _____

All about stories

Describing the seaside

Describing the seaside

♣ Look at this picture of the seaside. List as many words as you can in each box.

Sounds
you hear around you

The sea
how it looks, feels, things in it

Smells
from the sea and on the beach

The sand
how it looks, feels, things on it

Colours around you

♣ Describe the seaside in sentences. Try to use the words you have listed. Describe the sand, sea, smells, sounds and colours.

Teacher Timesavers: Story writing

21

All about stories

Name _____

Describing different characters

Describing different characters

✤ List words which describe each character.

	What they are doing	How they feel	How they look

Ideas

cycling

stamping

happy

cross

sad

old

young

reading

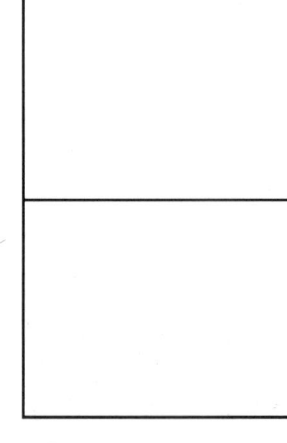

✤ Add some words of your own to each list.

Teacher Timesavers: Story writing

Name _____

All about stories
Describing a prince

Describing a prince

✤ Use the words in the box to help you describe the prince.

hair

shining

mouth

eyes

nose

body build

clothes

Describing words

happy   smart
blue   pointed
brown   long
thin   short
smiling   strong
curly   muscular
bright   expensive
shining   kind

✤ Choose a character of your own to describe on the back of this sheet.

Teacher Timesavers: Story writing

All about stories

Name _____

Good and bad characters

Good and bad characters

✤ List the words you would use to describe good and bad characters' personalities.

Good characters	Bad characters

Use the word box to help you.

Word box

evil	friendly	mean
kind	wicked	spiteful
helpful	hurtful	caring
cruel	good	sensitive
thoughtless	violent	nasty

✤ Try to add some more words of your own on the back of this sheet.

Name _____

All about stories
Events in stories

Events in stories

✤ Match each event with what could happen next.

Event   What could happen next

He escapes from the ghost and runs from the haunted house.

The plane crashes, but the pilot parachutes to safety.

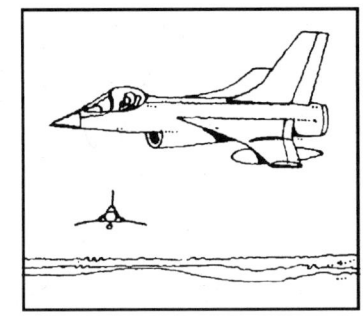

She is rescued by the walker on the cliff.

✤ Decide what could happen next for each of these events.

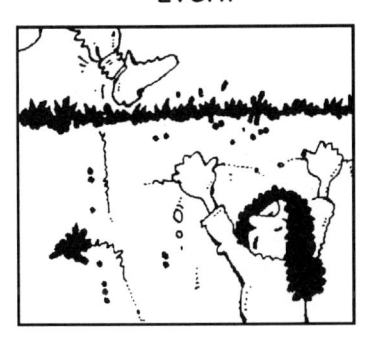

Teacher Timesavers: Story writing

25

All about stories

Name _____

Chain of events

Chain of events

✤ Complete this chain of events.

[dog image] → Victor the dog is hit by a car. → ◯ → ◯ → His owners collect him from the vet.

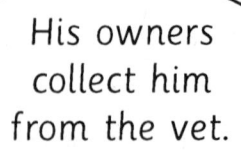

✤ Make a chain of events for these story openings.

[UFO over city image] → Aliens land in the city centre. → ◯ → ◯ → ◯

[forest image] → ◯ → ◯ → ◯ → ◯

✤ Make a chain of events for your own story opening.

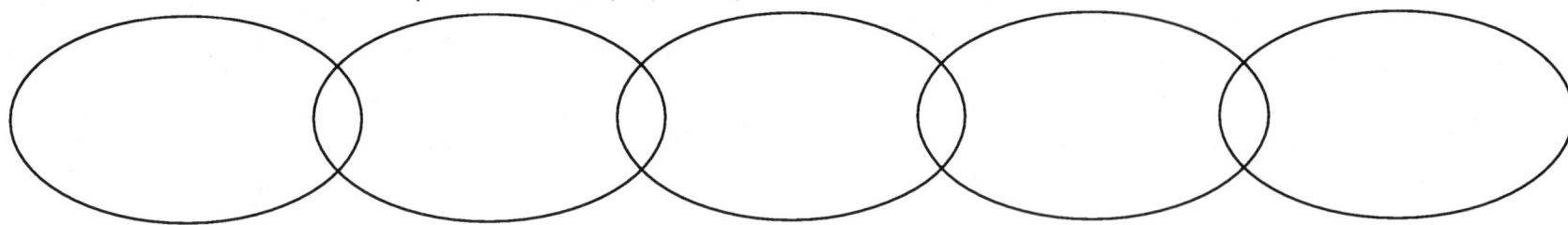

◯ → ◯ → ◯ → ◯ → ◯

Teacher Timesavers: Story writing

Name _____

All about stories
Ways to end stories

Ways to end stories

✤ Match each story ending with the way it is written.

> Some ways to end stories
> • sad ending
> • happy ending
> • happy ending and a new adventure starts

• Asha knew she would be allowed to keep the dog. She hugged her mum.

Way it ends _____

• The top of the mountain loomed before her. Jamie knew she had achieved her dream.

Way it ends _____

• Ryan and his father clambered into the van. 'Let the next trip begin,' Ryan said.

Way it ends _____

• Jack walked sadly towards the school gates. One tiny tear rolled down his cheek.

Way it ends _____

Teacher Timesavers: Story writing

All about stories

Name _____

Writing story endings

Writing story endings

✤ Write a story ending for each of these pictures.
Try to use the way of ending which is written beside each picture.

Way to end
Happy ending

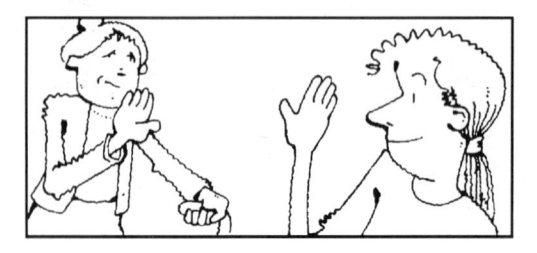

Way to end
Sad ending

Way to end
Happy ending and a new adventure starts

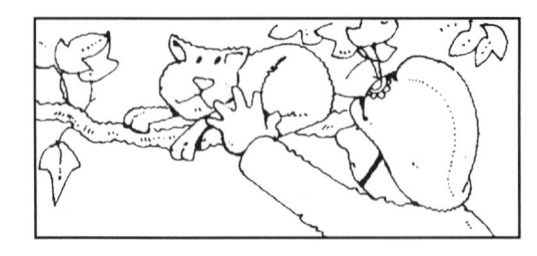

Way to end
Happy ending

28

Teacher Timesavers: Story writing

Name _____

Scary stories
Scary similes: 1

SCARY SIMILES: 1

A simile is a comparison between two things, using 'like' or 'as'.

For example: clear like glass, as red as the setting sun.

♣ Complete each phrase with a word from the ideas box.

- as old as _____
- as spooky as _____
- cold like _____

- dusty like _____
- as creepy as _____

♣ Think of some words of your own to complete each phrase below.

- as dark as _____
- loud like _____

- quiet like _____
- as still as _____

♣ Write a scary description of the castle in the picture. Use similes to help you.

Ideas

time

the snow

the desert

a cobweb

a haunted house

Teacher Timesavers: Story writing

29

Scary stories

Name _____

Scary similes: 2

SCARY SIMILES: 2

♣ Choose words to go in the spaces of this scary story opening.

In the dark sky the moon shone as white as _____. Kirsty shivered as she crept along the damp, dark corridor of the castle. The floor felt as cold as _____. Suddenly, from the darkness, she heard a noise. It was as loud as _____. Sparks of fear shot down Kirsty's back. Her legs trembled like _____. 'Don't worry!' whispered her friend, as softly as _____. 'It's only the wind rattling the windows.'

They stepped into the next room...

♣ Continue this story or write a scary simile story of your own.

30   Teacher Timesavers: Story writing

Name _____

Scary stories

Scary alliteration

SCARY ALLITERATION

Alliteration is when words that are next to or near each other start with the same letter.

For example: *black bat* or *sinister shape*.

♣ Match up these words to make alliterations.

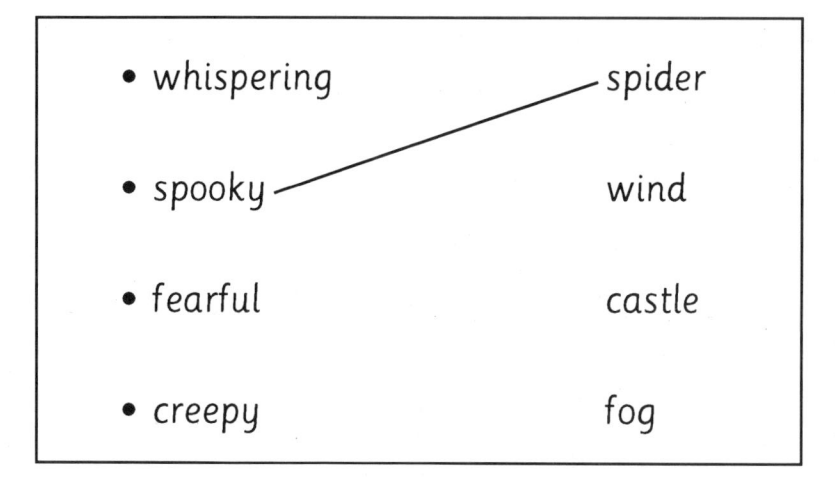

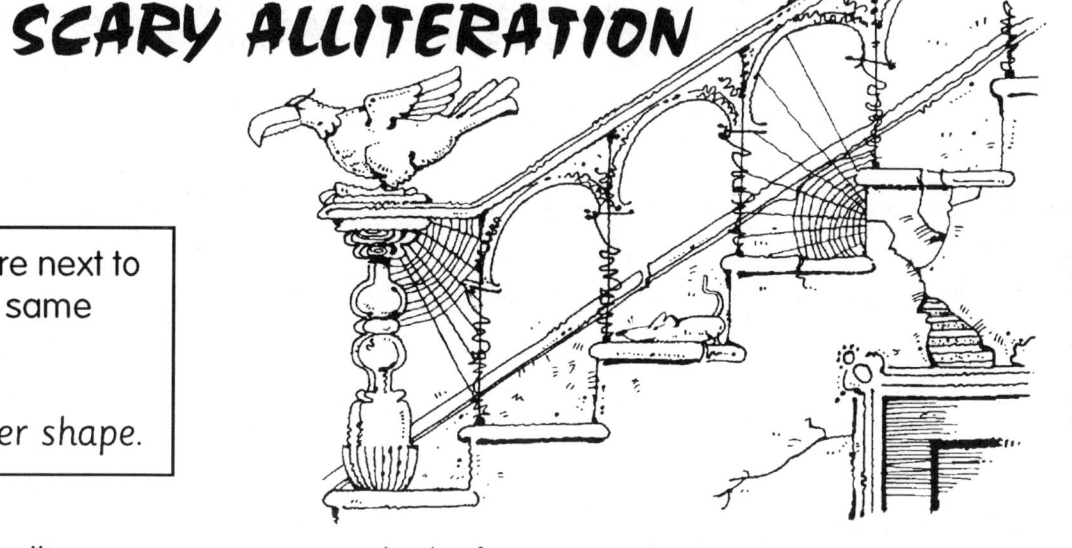

- whispering —— spider
- spooky ——/ wind
- fearful   castle
- creepy   fog

♣ Think of scary words to describe these objects. The words should start with the same letter.

Describing word	Object
squeaky	staircase
	mist
	night
	church
	tree

♣ Write a description of a scary place, using alliteration.

Teacher Timesavers: Story writing

31

Scary stories

Name _____

Scary story ingredients

SCARY STORY INGREDIENTS

♣ List scary ingredients in each box.

Scary places

old church

Scary objects

black cats

Scary sounds

screaming

Scary feelings

terror

Scary weather

wind

♣ Use a coloured pencil to highlight at least one word in each box that you will include in a scary story.

♣ Write your own scary story.

Teacher Timesavers: Story writing

Name _____

Scary stories

My monster

MY MONSTER

Drawing of monster

✤ You are going to make up a monster.
Fill in the spaces and tick the boxes which best describe it.

All about my monster

- My monster's name is _____
- My monster is   old ☐   young ☐
- My monster has   fur ☐   scales ☐   skin ☐
- My monster is   tall ☐   short ☐
- My monster is   male ☐   female ☐
- My monster   talks using my language ☐   grunts ☐
           talks with a language of its own ☐
- My monster moves quickly ☐   slowly ☐
- My monster is   friendly ☐ unfriendly ☐

- My monster lives in _____

- When people see my monster they will feel _____

_____

Teacher Timesavers: Story writing

Scary stories

Name _____

My monster story

MY MONSTER STORY

Choose one of the following monster story openings and continue the story.

- Icy mist swirled around the entrance to the cave.

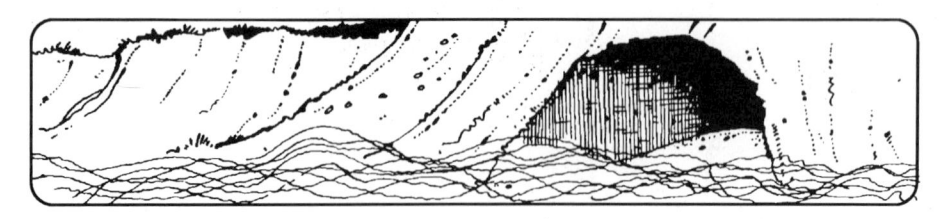

- Amanda sat up in bed feeling terrified. She was sure she could hear scurrying sounds outside.

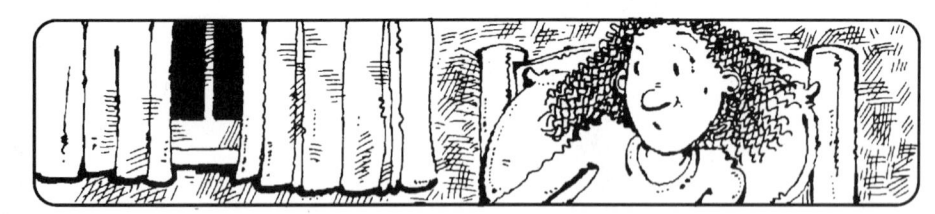

- Thud! Thud!
Two huge feet moved slowly through the long, wet grass.

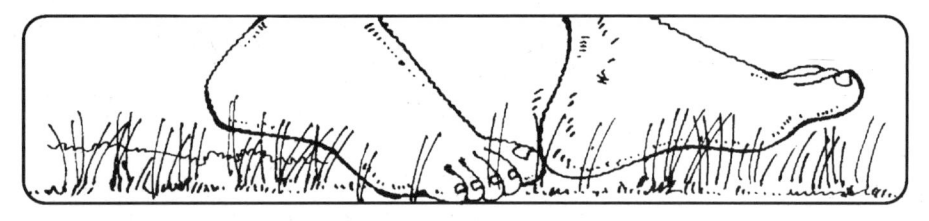

To think about

Where will your story be set?

Will the monster try to talk to people?

What will children think of the monster?

What will the monster eat?

Will the end of the story be happy or sad?

Teacher Timesavers: Story writing

Name _____

Animal stories

Safari animals

Safari animals

✤ Draw a line to match the words in the box to the right animal.

fast

dangerous

tall

heavy

✤ List some more words which describe each animal in the box.

Teacher Timesavers: Story writing

35

Animal stories

Safari story

Safari story

✤ Describe each animal and say what it is doing. The first one has been done for you.

The ____huge_____ elephant____ walked slowly towards the tree.____

The _____ giraffe _____

Two _____ lions _____

A _____ monkey _____

Some _____ cheetahs _____

Name _____

Animal stories

Animal opposites

Animal opposites

✤ List as many animals as you can think of under these headings.

large animals	small animals	land animals	sea animals	fast animals	slow animals

✤ Write a story about how two opposite animals make friends and help each other.

Teacher Timesavers: Story writing

🐾 Animal stories

Name _____

Creature feature

Creature feature

✤ Complete these creature features.

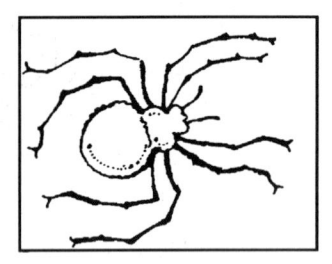

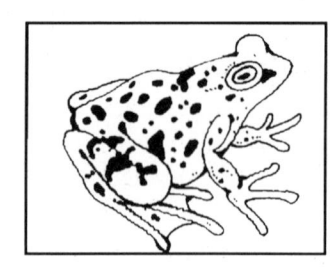

				Ideas
Type of creature	_____	_____	_____	soft fur
Where it lives	_____	_____	_____	croaking
How it looks	_____	_____	_____	bunnies
What it eats	_____	_____	_____	lettuce
What its babies are called	_____	_____	_____	flies
				warren

✤ Choose one of the creature features. Use it to help you write a description of the creature for the opening of an animal story. You could describe where it lives, how it looks and what it eats.

Teacher Timesavers: Story writing

Name _____

Animal stories

Reading an animal story

Reading an animal story

This is a story about a day in the life of Kevin the cool cat.

♣ Cut out the boxes and put them in the right order to tell the story.

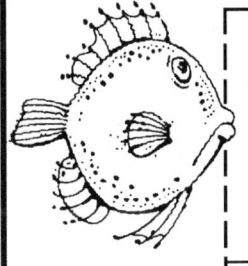

Kevin needed some breakfast. He found a small fish in the dustbin.	After breakfast Kevin met a tabby cat. The hair on Kevin's back stood on end in anger.
The scruffy tabby cat shot off into the distance. He knew he was on cool Kevin's territory.	It was a warm, sunny morning. Kevin the cool cat woke up and purred.
That night Kevin went out mouse-catching with his cool chums.	Kevin was tired after chasing the tabby cat. He slept all through the afternoon.

Teacher Timesavers: Story writing

39

Animal stories

Writing an animal story

Name _____

Writing an animal story

♣ Write a story which describes a whole day in the life of an animal.

♣ You could describe:

- how the animal looks
- where the animal lives
- how the animal gathers food
- the animal chasing or being chased by another animal

♣ Will your animal:

- have a name?
- be able to speak aloud?

Yes   No
☐   ☐
☐   ☐

♣ Draw pictures which show what happens in your story.

40

Teacher Timesavers: Story writing

Name _____

Animal stories
Animal tales

Animal tales

♣ Think of a story outline which would explain the following.

How the elephant got a long trunk

♣ Think of another story outline to explain an animal's features.

Why snakes hiss

How the zebra got its stripes

♣ Write the full story for one animal.

Teacher Timesavers: Story writing

41

🐾 *Animal stories*

Name _____

The chase

The chase

✤ Write a story about an animal which is being chased by humans. Plan your ideas below.

Which animal will you write about? _____

Why are humans chasing your animal? _____

Where will the chase take place? _____

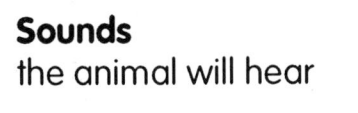

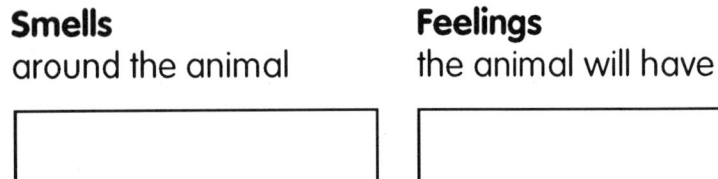

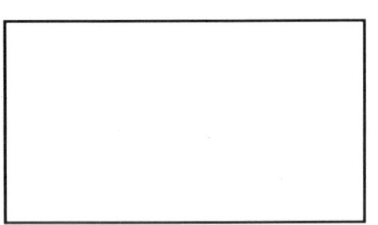

Sounds
the animal will hear

Smells
around the animal

Feelings
the animal will have

How will the story end? _____

✤ Use one of these starter lines for your story, or make up your own. Then write your story.

- The animal was petrified.
- The sun rose across the woodland.
- He could hear a strange sound in the distance.

42

Teacher Timesavers: Story writing

Name _____

Crime stories

Wanted poster

Wanted poster

✤ Complete this Wanted poster with details of an imaginary criminal and his or her crime.

Photofit picture

Wanted

Name _____
Alias _____
Age _____
Height _____
Hairstyle/hair colour _____
Eye colour _____
Clothes _____
_____
Crime _____
_____
Reward _____
If seen, telephone _____

Teacher Timesavers: Story writing

Crime stories

Name _____

Crime by numbers

Crime by numbers

✤ Roll a dice to find out which ingredients you will use in your story.

Objects	People	Crime	Place
⚀ rope	⚀ old man	⚀ shoplifting	⚀ local shops
⚁ car	⚁ young girl	⚁ breaking and entering	⚁ by a quiet canal
⚂ helicopter	⚂ teenager	⚂ stealing	⚂ an old church
⚃ glove	⚃ shop owner	⚃ forging a signature	⚃ prison
⚄ helmet	⚄ police officer	⚄ hurting someone	⚄ deserted castle
⚅ money	⚅ teacher	⚅ vandalism	⚅ seaside

a) Number _____

Object

_____

b) Number _____

Person

_____

c) Number _____

Crime

_____

d) Number _____

Place

_____

✤ Write your story using the ingredients you selected by rolling the dice.

44

Teacher Timesavers: Story writing

Name _____

Crime stories

Reporter's notebook

Reporter's notebook

✦ Make up the details of a crime. Pretend you are the reporter for a local newspaper and write about what happened.

- What crime occurred?
- Where did the crime take place?
- What time did it happen?
- Who was the victim of the crime?
- What did you find when you arrived on the scene?
- Were there any witnesses to the crime?
- How does the victim feel?
- Is there a description of the criminals?

Reporter

Teacher Timesavers: Story writing

Crime stories

Name _____

Burglary interview

Burglary interview

Imagine you are a reporter interviewing the victim of a burglary.
♣ Write down the victim's answers.

How did the burglar break in?

Please describe the damage the burglar caused.

Please describe what the burglar stole.

How did you feel when you realised you'd been burgled?

Did the burglar leave any evidence?

What do you think should happen to the burglar when he or she is caught?

Name _____

Crime stories

Headline news

Headline news

Newspaper headlines have to be short, simple and eye-catching.

♣ Write two different headlines for each of these crimes.

Headlines **Crime facts**

Two valuable vases were stolen from the city museum by masked robbers.

A brand new car was stolen from a garage in Gear Street. Police later discovered the car, which had been burned out.

♣ List possible crime facts for these newspaper headlines.

FOILED!   **VICTIM FIGHTS BACK!**

_____   _____
_____   _____
_____   _____
_____   _____
_____   _____
_____   _____
_____   _____
_____   _____
_____   _____

♣ Write a crime story in the form of a newspaper report. Try to include a newspaper headline, facts about the crime and a picture or photofit.

Teacher Timesavers: Story writing

47

Sports stories

Name _____

Football fun

Football fun

✤ Cut out these pictures. Put them in order to tell the story of the football match.

✤ Write what is happening under each picture.

48 Teacher Timesavers: Story writing

Name _____

Sports stories

Actions in sport

Actions in sport

♣ Describe each character's actions and explain how he or she is moving. The first one has been done for you.

| Emily | Nadir | Tom | Ruth | Katrina |

Emily ____danced____ across the floor ____gracefully.____

Nadir _____ around the track _____

Tom _____ over the hurdle _____

Ruth _____ to the end of the pool _____

Katrina _____ down the hill _____

Teacher Timesavers: Story writing

49

Sports stories

Characters in sport

Characters in sport

✤ Choose one sports character from the list below.

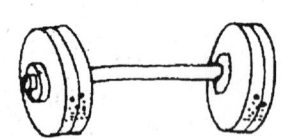

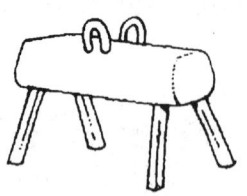

body-builder   Formula 1 champion   footballer   gymnast   ice-skater   100-metre runner

✤ Underline or highlight the words below that you think best describe your character.

body type	skills	mental attitude
athletic strong arms strong legs muscly tall short	strong quick thinking artistic speed body control sense of balance	determination concentration sense of fair play forward thinking positive desire to win

✤ Write a description of your character, and include more words which describe your character's body type, skills and mental attitude.

Teacher Timesavers: Story writing

Name _____

Sports stories

Problems in sport

Problems in sport

✤ List problems which characters could face in these sports events.

losing the ball

crashing

getting hurt

being knocked out

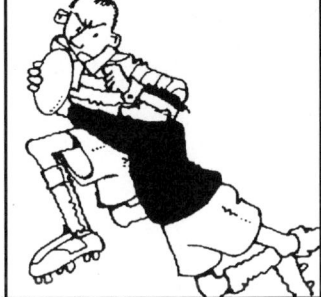

rugby

rallying

boxing

golf

engine failure

_____   _____   _____   _____
_____   _____   _____   _____
_____   _____   _____   _____
_____   _____   _____   _____
_____   _____   _____   _____

✤ Think of some more sporting problems for other sports.

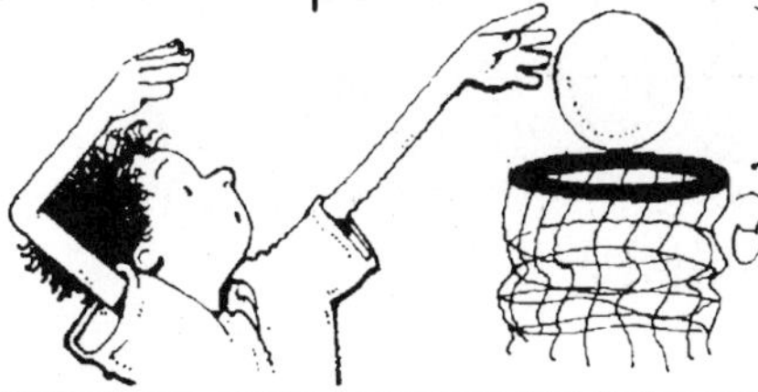

Teacher Timesavers: Story writing

Sports stories

Ordering chapter headings

Ordering chapter headings

The chapter headings below tell the story of Damian Mill and his Formula 1 race for the world championship.

♣ Reorder the chapter headings to tell Damian's story from start to finish.

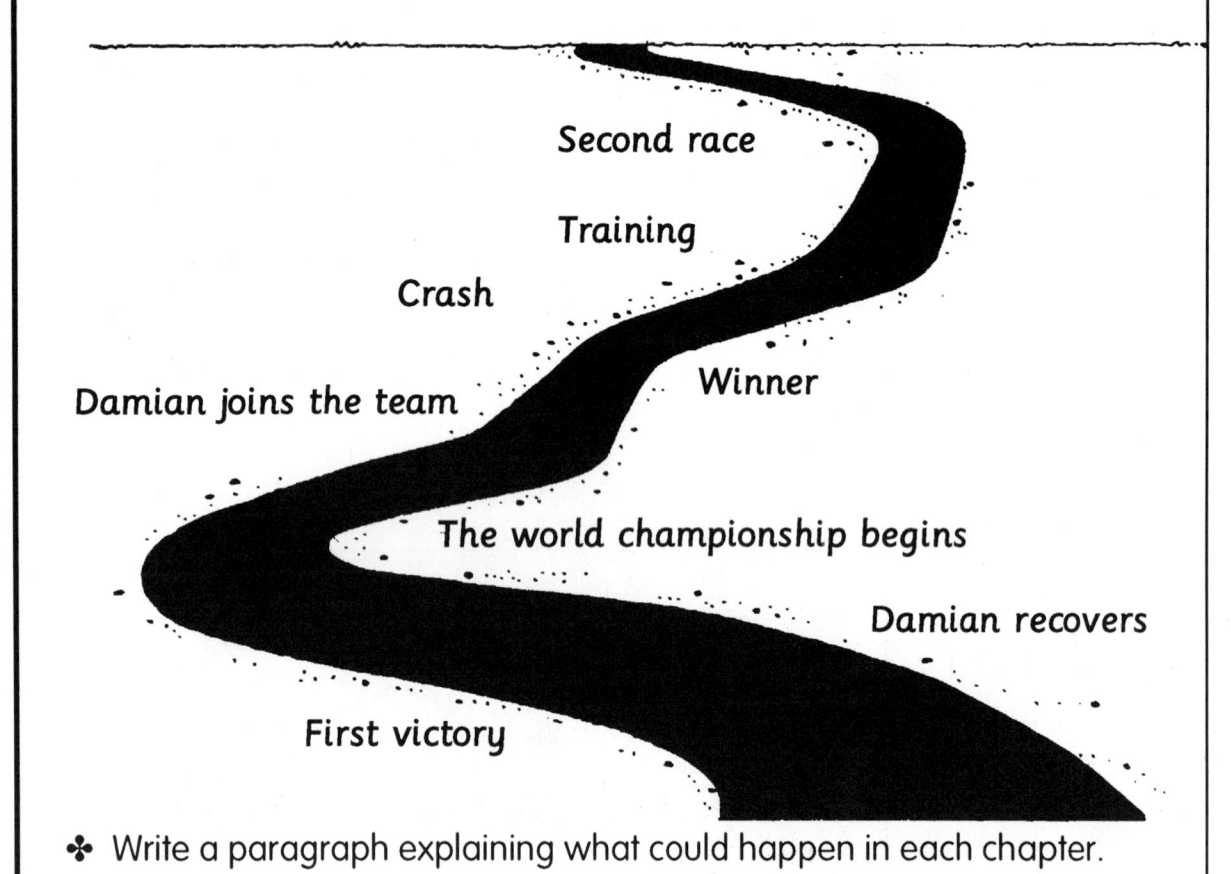

Second race
Training
Crash
Winner
Damian joins the team
The world championship begins
Damian recovers
First victory

1. Damian joins the team.
2.
3.
4.
5.
6.
7.
8.

♣ Write a paragraph explaining what could happen in each chapter.

Teacher Timesavers: Story writing

Name _____

Sports stories

Writing chapter headings

Writing chapter headings

Story outline

1. Zoë wants to play tennis. She gets into the British team.

2. Her parents realise that they don't have enough money to support her training. A local firm offers to sponsor her.

3. Zoë wins her first big match.

4. During her second match Zoë collapses.

5. Doctors are sure she'll never play tennis again. A new treatment is found.

6. Zoë recovers, retrains and goes on to win the British championship for the under 15s.

♣ Read the story outline.

♣ Write six chapter headings to explain what happens in each chapter.

Chapter headings

1. _____

2. _____

3. _____

4. _____

5. _____

6. _____

♣ Think of alternative chapter headings for each chapter.

Teacher Timesavers: Story writing

53

Sports stories

Name _____

Sport story

Sport story

✣ Choose a sport story title or make up one of your own.

| Football fever | Ace | Championship dreams | Your idea _____ |

✣ Write four chapter headings for your title. Write a list of the events in each chapter.

Chapter headings

1.

2.

3.

4.

Events

1.

2.

3.

4.

✣ Write the first chapter of your story.

Teacher Timesavers: Story writing

Name _____

Sports stories

Sports commentators

Sports commentators

♣ Write what each commentator is saying beside these pictures.

♣ Tell the story of a match or race by writing what the commentator said.

Teacher Timesavers: Story writing

Sports stories

Name _____

The competition

The competition

✤ Write a story where your main character takes part in a sports competition. Use this sheet to plan your ideas.

Sport

Competition

Setting

Events in the story

Character

body type   skills   mental attitude

Ending
What will happen?

Teacher Timesavers: Story writing

Name _____

Adventure stories

John's journey

John's journey

♣ Write one or two sentences under the pictures to explain what happened to John.

John set off.

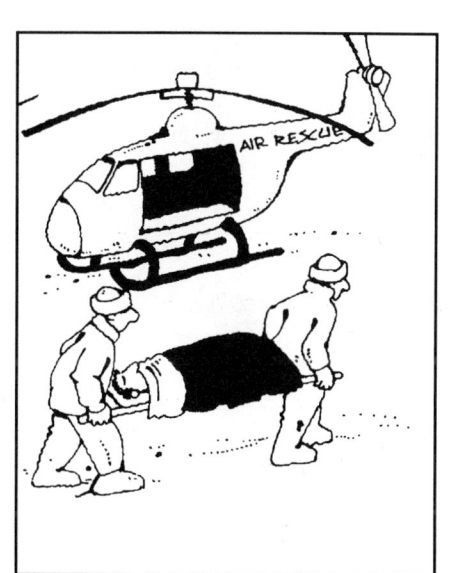

♣ Write what happened to John when he arrived at the hospital.

Teacher Timesavers: Story writing

57

Adventure stories

Jungle adventure

Jungle adventure

Kate is an explorer who travelled through the jungle.

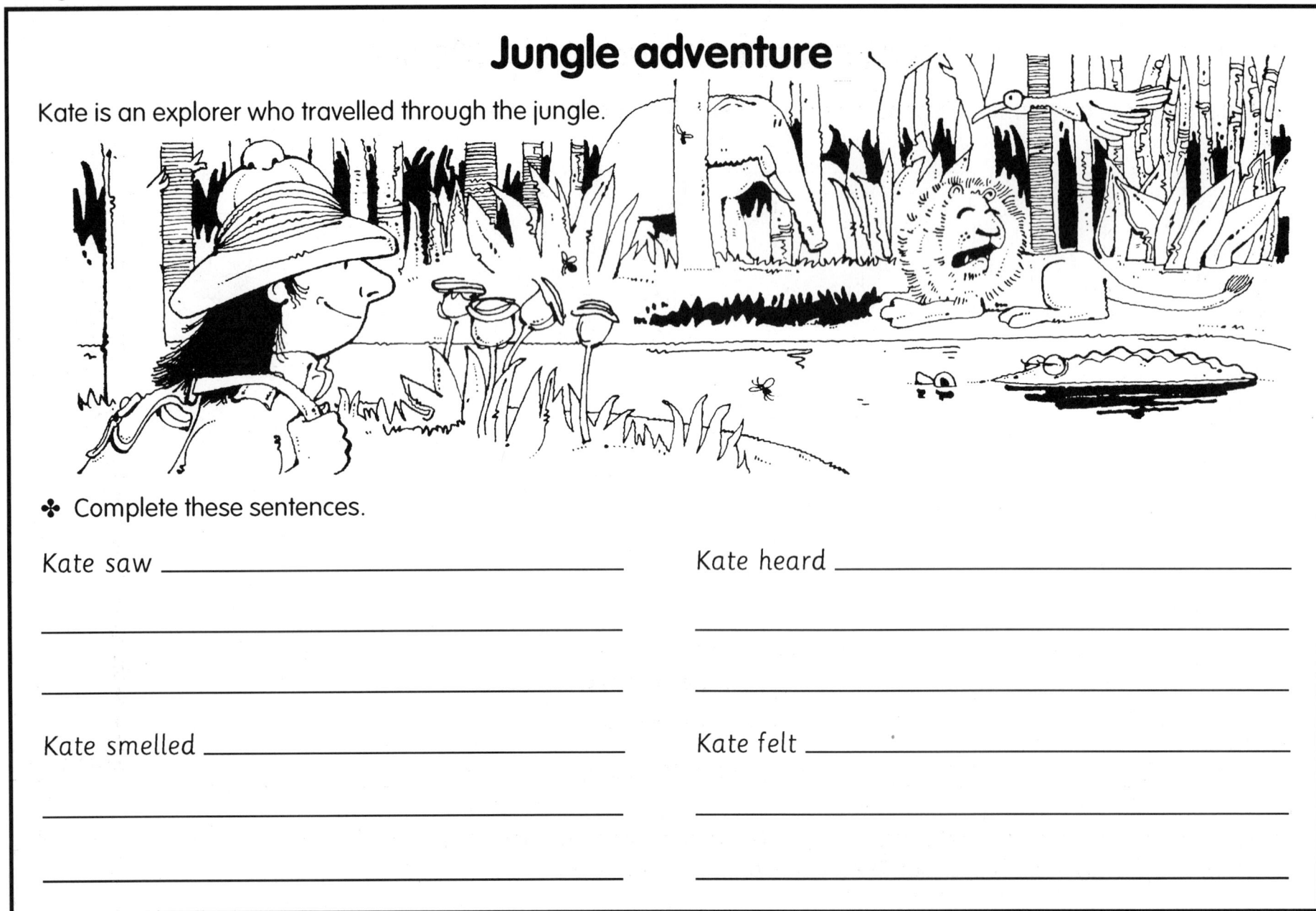

✣ Complete these sentences.

Kate saw _____

_____

_____

Kate smelled _____

_____

_____

Kate heard _____

_____

_____

Kate felt _____

_____

_____

Teacher Timesavers: Story writing

Name _____

Adventure stories

Characters in adventure stories

Characters in adventure stories

✤ List words which describe the behaviour and personalities of adventure story heroes/heroines and villains.

Heroes and heroines	Ideas	Villains
	helpful selfish unkind determined inconsiderate devious cowardly thoughtful trustworthy hurts others helps others never gives up	

✤ Describe a hero/heroine and a villain from an adventure story you have read or seen. Write about their behaviour, personality and what they do.

Teacher Timesavers: Story writing

Adventure stories Name _____

Adventure story chart

Adventure story chart

♣ Choose one adventure story that you know.
Fill in the chart.

Name of the adventure story	
Name of the hero or heroine	
Describe the clothes the hero/heroine wears.	
Name of the villain	
Describe the clothes the villain wears.	
Where is the story set?	
Why does the hero/heroine set off on the adventure?	
How does the adventure end?	
Did you enjoy watching, listening to or reading the adventure story? Why?	

Name _____

Adventure stories

Story ingredients

Story ingredients

✤ Plan ideas for the ingredients of your own adventure story.

Hero/heroine

Name _____

Age _____

Personality _____

Clothes worn _____

_____

Equipment _____

_____

Reason for the adventure

save the world ☐   other ☐

catch an evil villain ☐   _____

find a valuable object ☐

Villain

Name _____

Transport

on foot ☐   plane ☐

jeep ☐   other ☐
_____

Setting

jungle ☐   city ☐   mountains ☐

sea ☐   desert ☐   other ☐
_____

✤ Write the adventure story using the above ingredients.

Teacher Timesavers: Story writing

61

Adventure stories

Exploration adventure

Exploration adventure

You are going to write a story in which your hero or heroine explores an exciting, dangerous place.

♣ Choose a place for your character to explore.

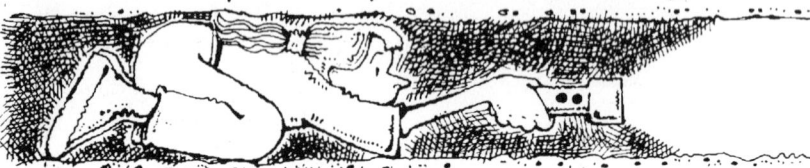

mountain range ☐   tropical island ☐

Arctic Circle ☐   other _____

♣ Plan ideas for some problems which your character will come across during his or her exploration.

Ideas

trapped by snow
having to cross a river with no bridge
attacked by a snake
fear of heights
losing the compass
running out of food

♣ Explain how your character will solve the problems.

Problems	Solutions

♣ Write your exploration adventure. Don't forget to describe the setting. Show your character solving the problems he or she is faced with.

62   Teacher Timesavers: Story writing

Name _____

Fairy stories
Fairy stories list

Fairy stories list

♣ Complete the chart below using fairy stories you know.

Story title	Good characters	Bad characters	Setting
_____	_____	_____	_____
_____	_____	_____	_____
_____	_____	_____	_____
_____	_____	_____	_____
_____	_____	_____	_____
_____	_____	_____	_____
_____	_____	_____	_____
_____	_____	_____	_____

Aladdin

Little Red Riding Hood

Jack and the Beanstalk

Goldilocks and the Three Bears

Teacher Timesavers: Story writing

63

Fairy stories

Name _____

Writing fairy story openings

Writing fairy story openings

✤ Choose one good character, one bad character and one setting from the lists below. Write the ingredients you have chosen below each column.

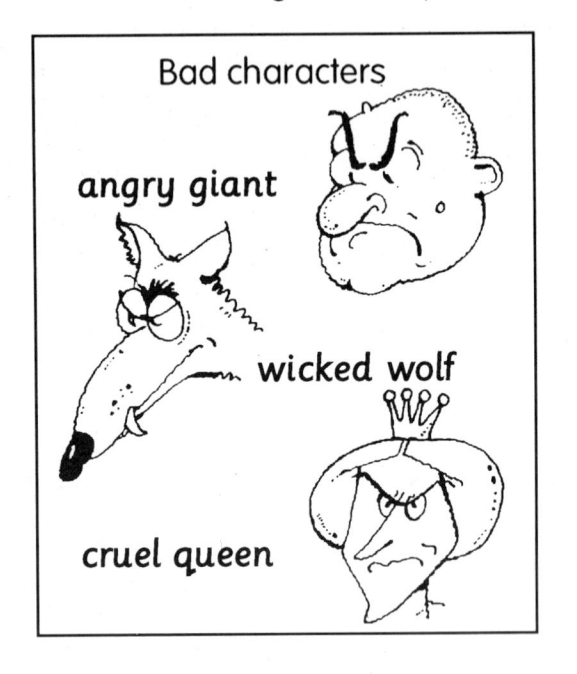

Bad characters
- angry giant
- wicked wolf
- cruel queen

Good characters
- poor young girl
- sad prince
- wise old woman

Setting
- old castle
- small cottage
- dark forest

Bad character _____ Good character _____ Setting _____

✤ Write three different openings for a fairy story using your chosen characters and setting.
- Opening 1 – describe your good character.
- Opening 2 – write a conversation between your good and bad characters.
- Opening 3 – describe the setting.

Teacher Timesavers: Story writing

Name _____

Fairy stories

Jack and the Beanstalk

Jack and the Beanstalk

✤ Cut out these squares. Put them in the right order to tell the story of Jack and the Beanstalk.

At the top of the beanstalk Jack discovered	When Jack returned with the beans, his mum	Quickly, Jack climbed down the beanstalk. Then he
When the giant saw Jack he	Jack climbed the beanstalk which	Jack swapped his cow for some magic

✤ Complete the unfinished sentences.

Teacher Timesavers: Story writing

65

Fairy stories

Name _____

Little Red Riding Hood

Little Red Riding Hood

♣ Write what Little Red Riding Hood and the wolf are saying to each other in the speech bubbles.

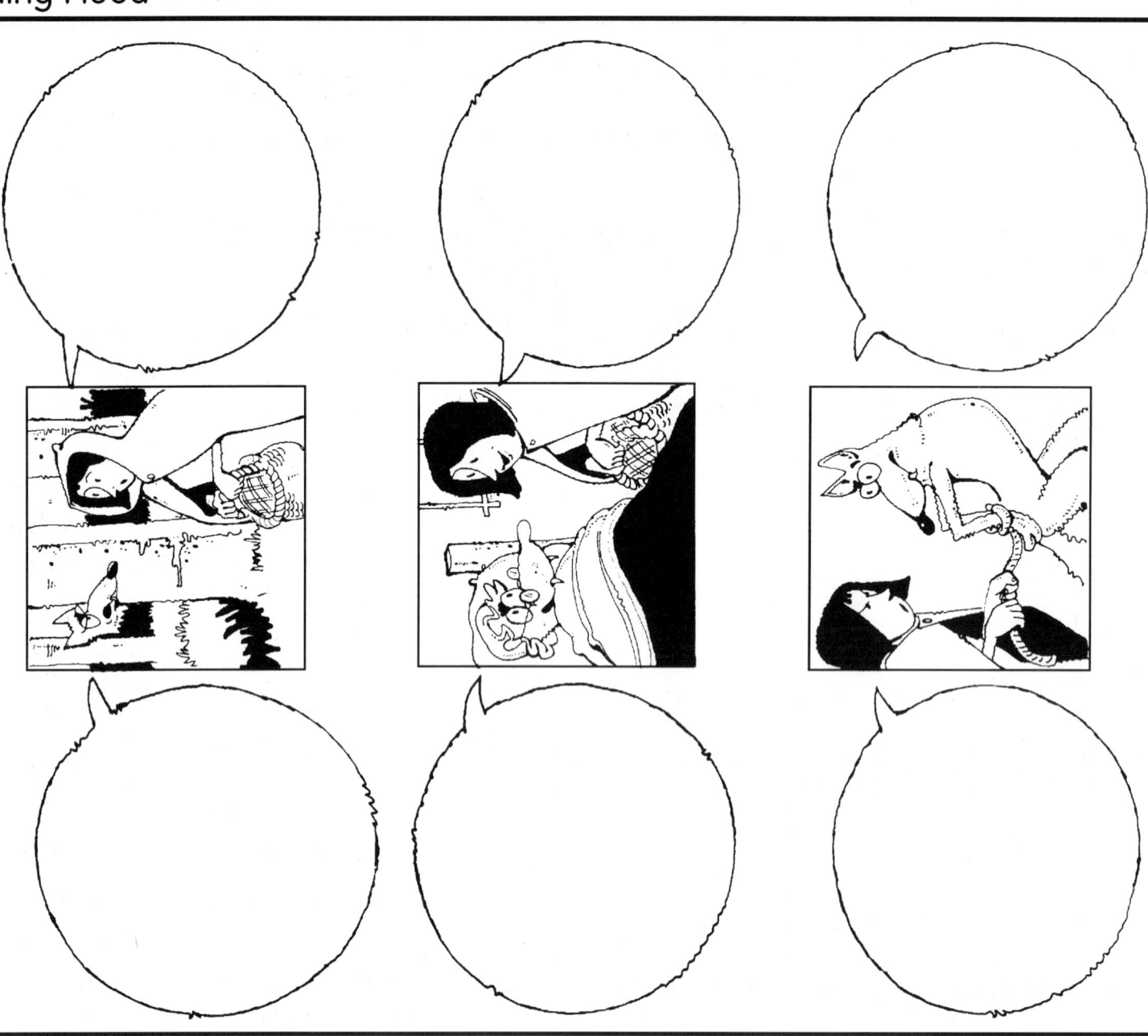

♣ Retell the story of Little Red Riding Hood in your own words.

66 Teacher Timesavers: Story writing

Name _____

Fairy stories

Making fairy stories modern: 1

Making fairy stories MODERN: 1

This chart shows you how to take the ingredients from a fairy story and make them modern.

Cinderella

old ingredients	modern ingredients
Cinderella	Gemma
pumpkin that turns into a coach	

Cinderella

Gemma

✤ Write old and modern ingredients on the chart.

✤ List some more modern ingredients on the back of this sheet.

Ideas

magic slipper   broom   ballgown

Teacher Timesavers: Story writing

67

Fairy stories

Making fairy stories modern: 2

Making fairy stories MODERN: 2

♣ List four ingredients from a fairy story you know. Then try to think of four modern ingredients that could replace these. Use the bags of ideas if you need help.

Name of fairy story _____	
old ingredients	modern ingredients

♣ Write your own modern fairy story, using the modern ingredients on your chart.

Name _____

Fairy stories

Leon and the Sad Giant

Leon and the Sad Giant

✣ Write what you think Leon and the Sad Giant are saying to each other in the speech bubbles.

✣ Write what Leon and the Sad Giant are saying as direct speech below each picture. Remember to use speech marks.

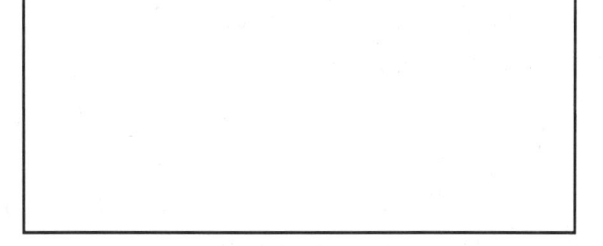

✣ Use the back of this sheet to tell the story of Leon and the Sad Giant in your own words.

Teacher Timesavers: Story writing

69

Fairy stories

Different endings

Name _____

Different endings

♣ Write a different ending for each of these fairy stories. Your ending could be funny, sad or just different! Plan your ideas first below.

Goldilocks and the Three Bears

How it really ends

My idea

Sleeping Beauty

How it really ends

My idea

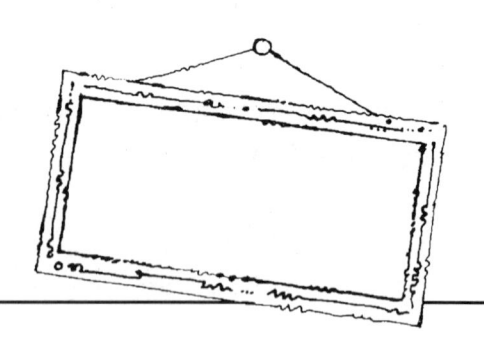

A fairy story of my own choice

_____

How it really ends

My idea

Teacher Timesavers: Story writing

Name _____

Real-life stories

How I felt

How I felt

✤ Think about how different events made you feel.
Then complete these sentences.

I felt happy when _____

I felt sad when _____

I laughed when _____

I felt angry when _____

I felt scared when _____

I felt excited when _____

✤ Make up a main character and write a story which shows how the character felt as a result of something which happened to him or her. Use your own experience as the starting point for your story.

Ideas

Teacher Timesavers: Story writing

Real-life stories

This is my life

Name _____

This is my life

✤ Write a description of one event in your life that you remember well.

✤ Which event will you choose?   ✤ Plan your writing by making notes below.

- happy event
- sad event
- embarrassing event
- scary event
- other
- _____

Describe:
- where you were
- who was with you
- exactly what happened
- how you felt and why
- how old you were

✤ Now write your description.

Teacher Timesavers: Story writing

Name _____

Real-life stories

Feelings can change

Feelings can change

✣ Think about how each character might feel before and after the events below.

Character	Feelings about the event when they are waiting for it to happen	Event	Feelings after the event has happened
		Baby brother is born.	
		She retires.	
		His best friend moves away.	
		They get a new pet.	

Ideas

happiness
sadness
anger
love
hurt
fear
jealousy
hope
excitement
peace
acceptance
worry
loneliness

✣ Choose one character and event from above. Write a story showing how your character feels before and after the event and why.

Teacher Timesavers: Story writing

73

Real-life stories

Name _____

Friendship story

Friendship story

♣ Work with a friend in your class. Make notes about your friendship.

My friend's name is	My friend's age is	What my friend looks like	What my friend and I first thought of each other and why	How and when my friend and I first met	My friend's special qualities are

♣ Tell the story of your friendship. Use the notes you have made to help you to write your story.

74

Teacher Timesavers: Story writing

Name _____

Real-life stories
Friends and enemies

Friends and enemies

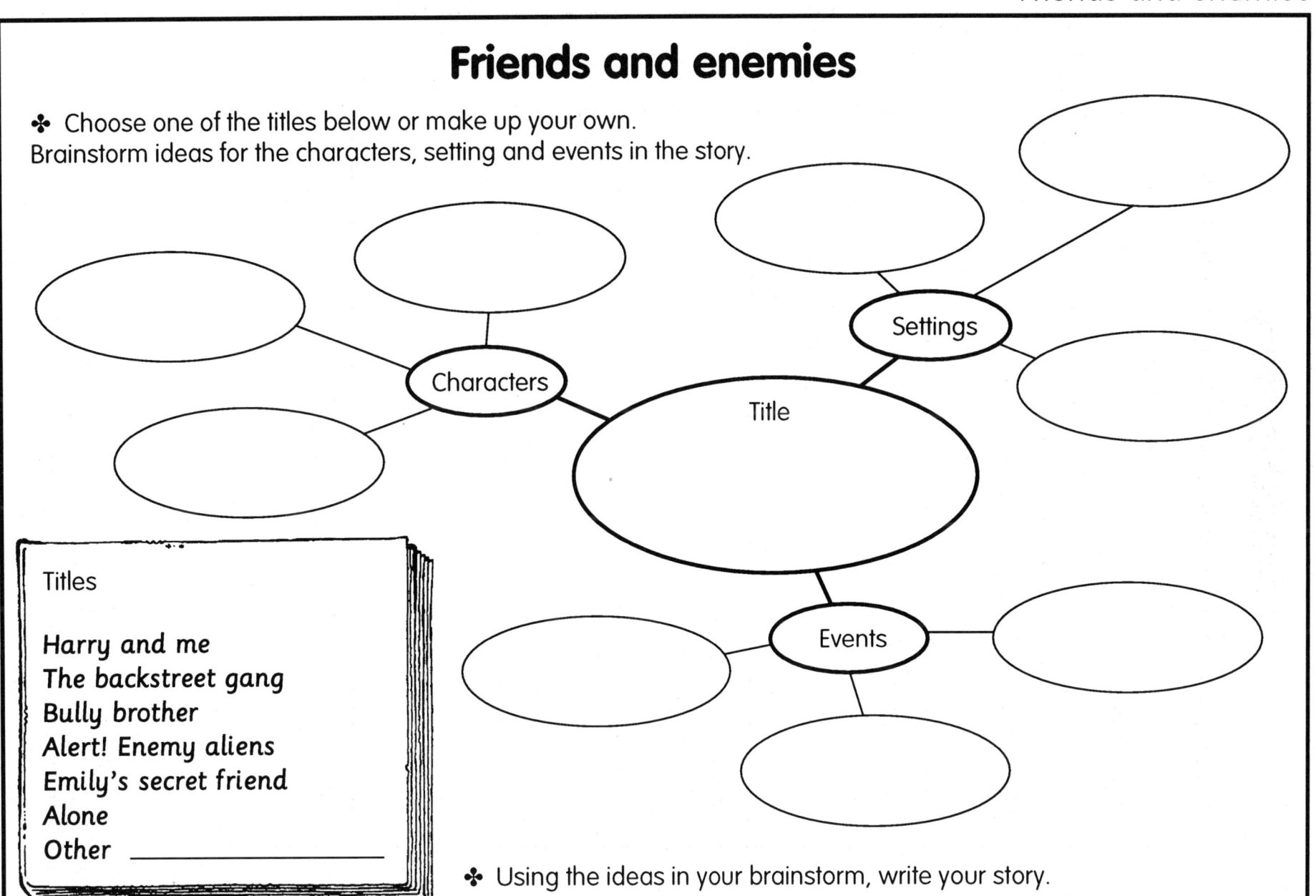

✤ Choose one of the titles below or make up your own.
Brainstorm ideas for the characters, setting and events in the story.

(Characters) — (Title) — (Settings)
                  |
               (Events)

Titles

Harry and me
The backstreet gang
Bully brother
Alert! Enemy aliens
Emily's secret friend
Alone
Other _____

✤ Using the ideas in your brainstorm, write your story.

Teacher Timesavers: Story writing

Real-life stories

Name _____

Which person?

Which person?

I could not stop laughing. Tears were pouring down my cheeks.

Ben could not stop laughing. Tears were pouring down his cheeks.

1st person narrative   **3rd person narrative**

♣ Decide whether these story openings are told in the first or third person. Tick the correct box.

Leah stormed through the doorway. She stopped in front of the sofa and glowered angrily at her brother.

☐ 1st person narrative   ☐ 3rd person narrative

I guess it was just one of those things. I know I shouldn't really have lost my temper.

☐ 1st person narrative   ☐ 3rd person narrative

They were all laughing, laughing at her.

☐ 1st person narrative   ☐ 3rd person narrative

I heard every word he said from my hiding place.

☐ 1st person narrative   ☐ 3rd person narrative

The doorbell rang. Mike ignored it. The bell rang again. Mike sighed and stopped playing the game on his computer. 'This had better be important!' he muttered.

☐ 1st person narrative   ☐ 3rd person narrative

♣ Choose one story opening written in the third person. Rewrite the opening in the first person and continue the story.

Name _____

Real-life stories

New situations

New situations

✤ List the people, events and feelings which are associated with these places.

school		dentist	
	people		people
	events		events
	feelings		feelings

hospital		swimming pool	
	people		people
	events		events
	feelings		feelings

✤ Use your list to write a story for young children which is set in one of the above places.
The purpose of writing the story is to reassure and prepare a young child for his or her first visit to your chosen place.

Teacher Timesavers: Story writing

Space stories

Name _____

Space journey

Space journey

✤ Write what these characters are saying inside the speech bubbles.

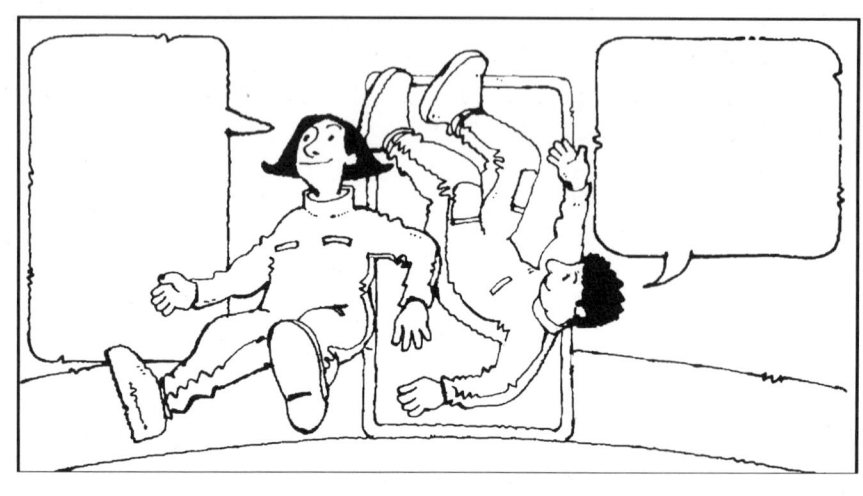

✤ Write what happened next in your own words.

78   Teacher Timesavers: Story writing

Name _____

Space stories

My pen-pal's an alien!

My pen-pal's an alien!

Imagine that you are working on a computer in school. Suddenly a message appears on your screen. It is from an alien who lives on the planet Rizlo.
✤ List the questions you will ask the alien about itself and its planet.

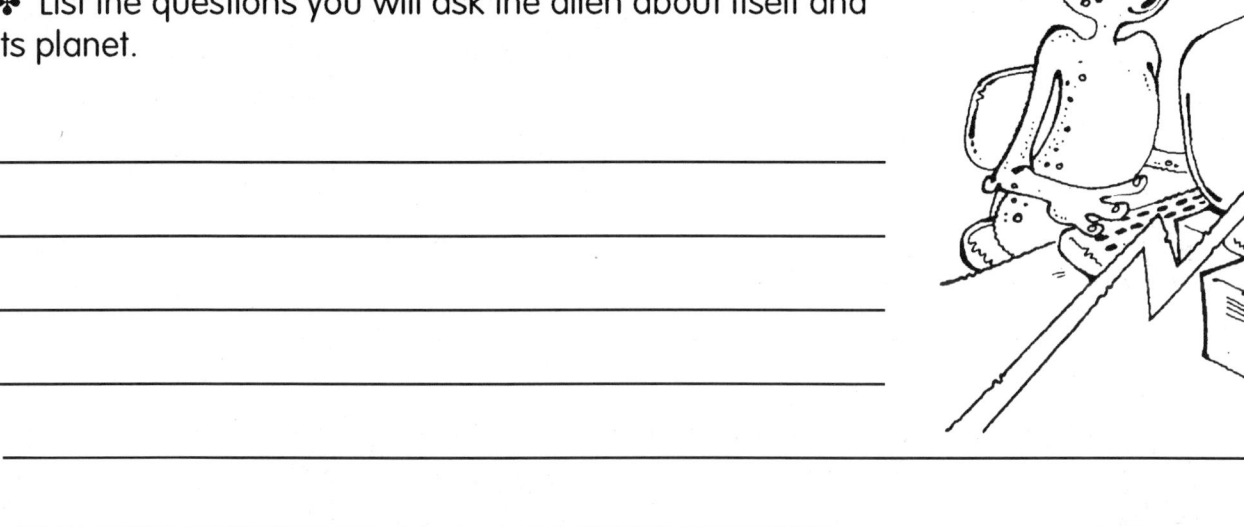

_____
_____
_____
_____
_____
_____
_____
_____

Ideas

Where do you live?
Is your planet polluted?
Describe what you do each day.

✤ Now make up some answers to the questions as if you are the alien.

Teacher Timesavers: Story writing

Space stories

Name _____

Alien visitor

Alien visitor

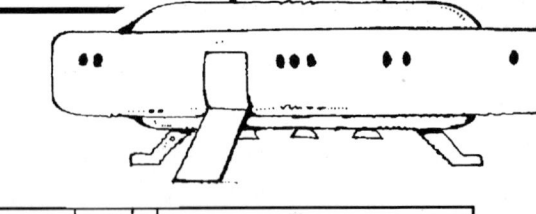

✤ Explain what is happening and what could happen next in each picture.

✤ Write the complete story of an alien's visit.

Teacher Timesavers: Story writing

Name _____

Space stories

Astronaut file

Astronaut file

Imagine you are an astronaut who is applying to become the first person on Earth to journey to a newly discovered planet in outer space.

♣ Fill in the details about yourself on this astronaut-file application form.

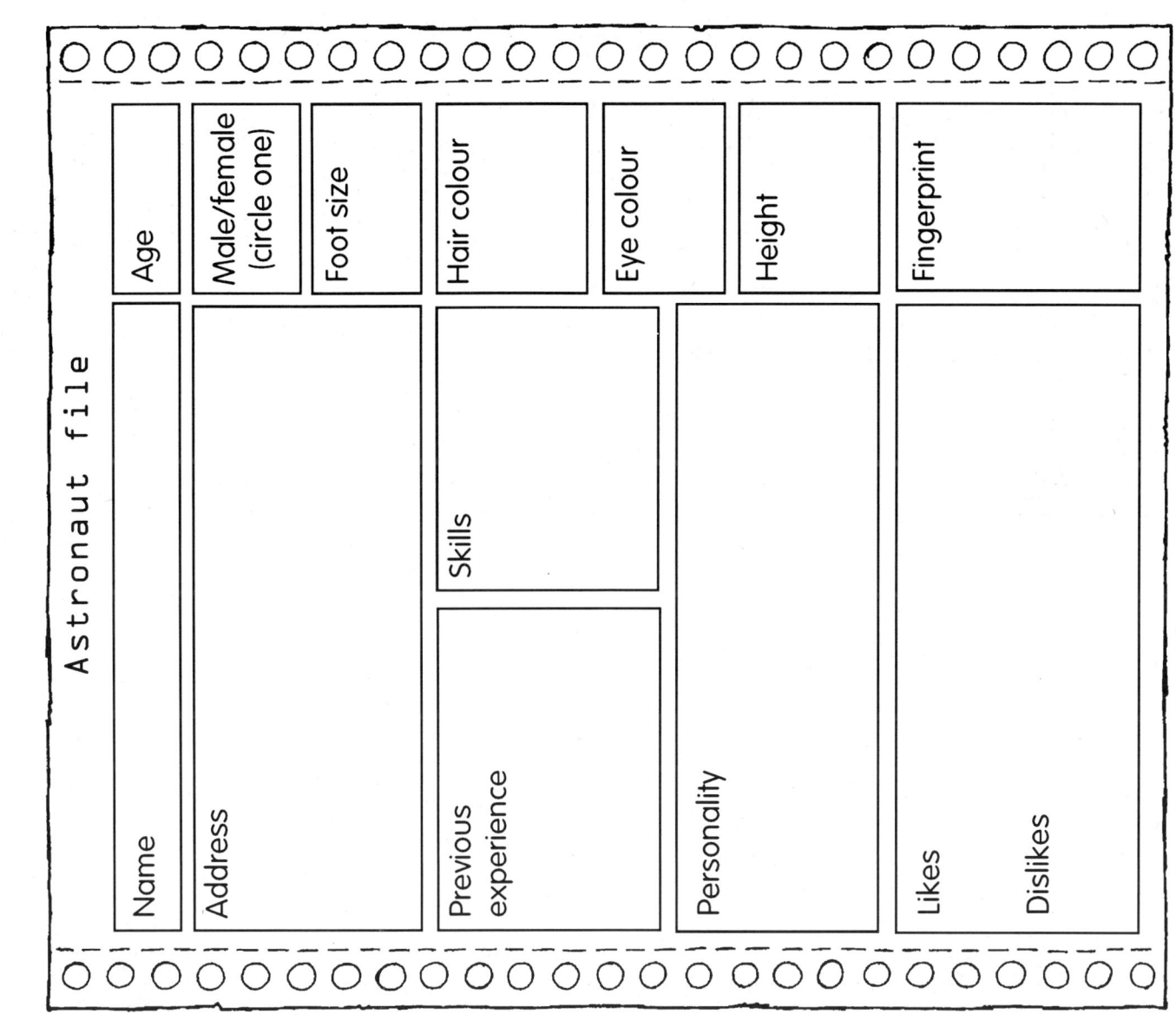

Astronaut file

- Name
- Address
- Age
- Male/female (circle one)
- Foot size
- Hair colour
- Skills
- Previous experience
- Eye colour
- Height
- Personality
- Fingerprint
- Likes
- Dislikes

♣ On the back of this sheet make a list of reasons why you think you are the best person for this job.

Teacher Timesavers: Story writing

Space stories

Name _____

Blast off!

Blast off!

Imagine you are an astronaut.
✤ Write a description of what happened when your rocket blasted off into space.

- Time of take-off

- Destination

- Description of the blast-off

- Description of what you could see and how you felt as the rocket travelled away from Earth

Ideas
sounds
smells
feelings
events
colours
sights
objects

✤ Write a description of the rest of your journey.

Teacher Timesavers: Story writing

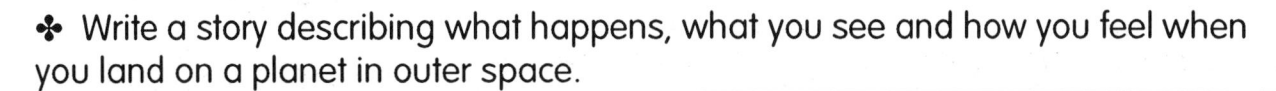

Name _____

Space stories

On the planet

On the planet

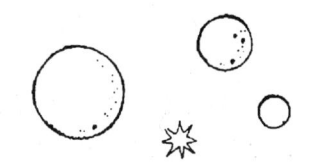

✤ Write a story describing what happens, what you see and how you feel when you land on a planet in outer space.

Use one of the story openings in the boxes.

| I was thrown forwards as the rocket landed. I got up and pressed the button to open the rocket door. It opened slowly. | The dust settled as the rocket engines shut down. My heart pounded. I didn't know what I would find outside. |

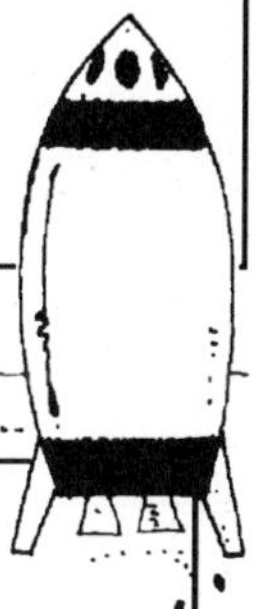

♣ Make notes before you start your story.

| Describe what you see around you when the rocket door opens.

Explain what the beings on the planet do when they see you. | Say how you try to communicate with the beings.

Describe where you go and explain what happens to you. |

Teacher Timesavers: Story writing

83

Space stories

Name _____

The message

The message

Imagine you are the commander of a spaceship. As you and your crew are passing a planet a message appears on your ship's screen.

✤ Use the key below to help you write down the first two words of the message in English on the screen.

a	○	h	l	o	⌗	v	∪
b	∩	i	∞	p	⚭	w	✻
c	—	j	☐	q	☆	x	∷
d	∧	k	∕	r	<	y	Ϻ
e	∀	l	\	s	Ǝ	z	◁▷
f	╬	m	∨	t	𐊧		
g	2	n	⋀	u	⊢		

Planet's language 2<∀∀⚭∞⋀2Ǝ/∀○<⚭l\∞⋀2⟨

English _____ _____

✤ Make up the rest of the message.

Planet's language

_____

English

_____

Will it be
• a threat?
• a cry for help?
• an invitation to visit?

✤ Tell the story of what happens next.

84   Teacher Timesavers: Story writing

Name _____

Space stories

○ Planet in danger story

Planet in danger story

♣ List the possible effects of each of these planetary problems.

Try to suggest one way in which each problem could be solved.

Food starts to run out

Effects

Solution

A strange disease breaks out

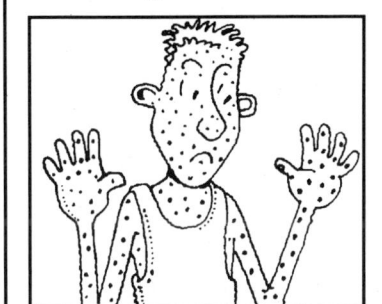

Effects

Solution

Poisonous fumes start to poison the air

Effects

Solution

Attack by another planet

Effects

Solution

♣ Write a story about a problem faced by beings on a planet. Describe what effects the problem causes and how the beings solve the problem.

Teacher Timesavers: Story writing

85

School stories

Name _____

In the morning

✤ Draw an arrow from the characters to the description of what they are doing and where they are. Use the picture to help you.

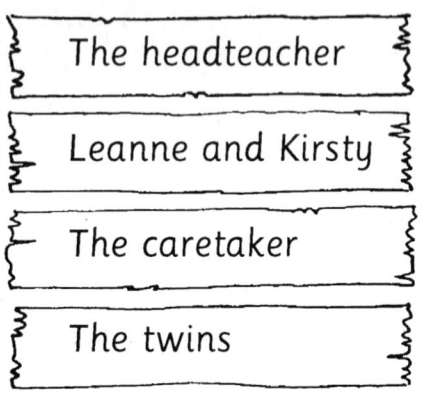

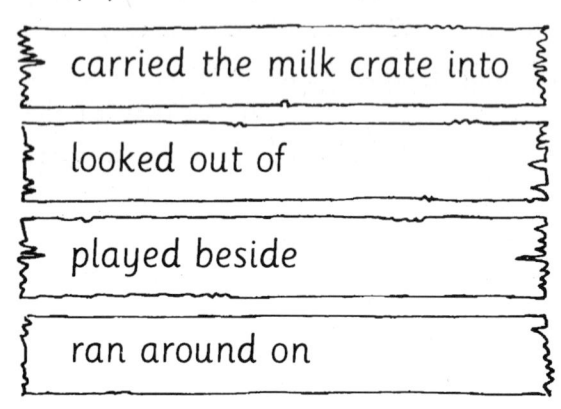

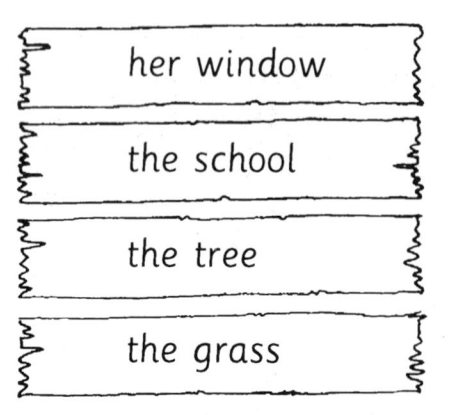

The headteacher	carried the milk crate into	her window
Leanne and Kirsty	looked out of	the school
The caretaker	played beside	the tree
The twins	ran around on	the grass

✤ Write about what you see and what happens when you arrive at school each morning.

86

Teacher Timesavers: Story writing

Name _____

School stories
School record files

School record files

♣ Read the school record file below.

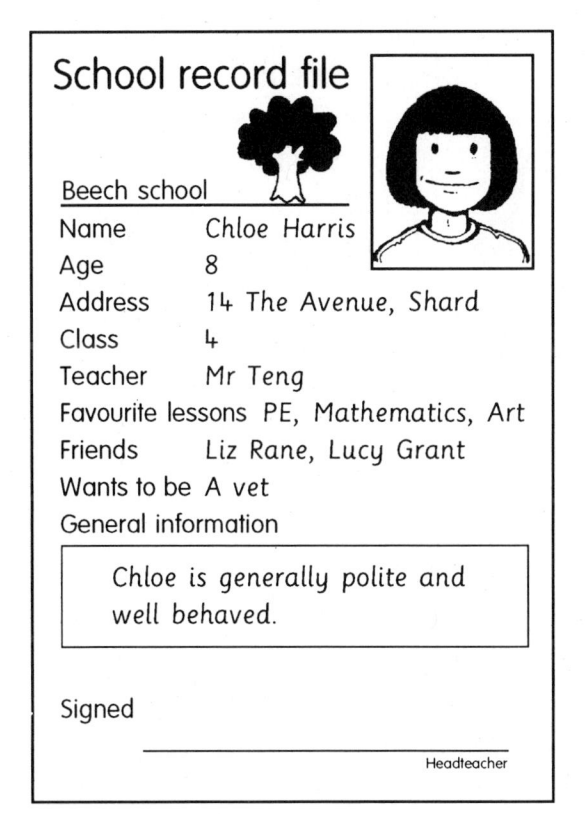

♣ Invent your own character and write down his or her details on the school record file below.

School record file

Beech school

Name   Chloe Harris
Age   8
Address 14 The Avenue, Shard
Class   4
Teacher Mr Teng
Favourite lessons PE, Mathematics, Art
Friends Liz Rane, Lucy Grant
Wants to be A vet
General information

> Chloe is generally polite and well behaved.

Signed
_____
Headteacher

♣ Write a description of your character, including the information on his or her school record file.

School record file

Name _____
Age _____
Address _____
_____
Class _____
Teacher _____
Favourite lessons _____
Friends _____
Wants to be _____
General information

Signed
_____
Headteacher

Teacher Timesavers: Story writing

87

School stories

Problems in school

Name _____

Problems in school

✤ Look at the events below which have caused problems for each character. List how you think each character might feel as a result of his or her problem.

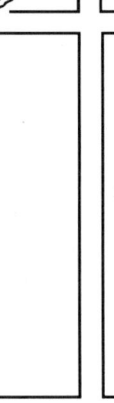

Problem 1 Rebecca forgot her lunch-box	**Problem 2** William argued with his friend	**Problem 3** Jade was bullied by an older pupil	**Problem 4** Marcus didn't understand the new maths work

✤ Write down one thing each character could do to try to solve his or her problem.

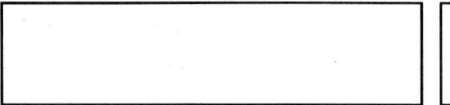

✤ On the back of this sheet list some more school problems characters might have to face.

Teacher Timesavers: Story writing

Name _____

School stories

A teacher's day

A teacher's day

✤ Make a storyboard of the events in a teacher's day.
Write your ideas or draw pictures in each box.

			Ideas
before school	morning lessons	playtime	
lunchtime	afternoon lessons	after school	

✤ Use your storyboard to help you to write a story describing the events in a teacher's day.

Teacher Timesavers: Story writing

89

School stories

Finding out about school

Finding out about school

✣ Make a list of as many words as you can in the boxes below.

Sounds around school	Smells around school	Objects around school	People around school

✣ Write a story about what happens to a new pupil on his or her first day at a new school. Remember to describe sounds, smells and objects as well as the people he or she meets.

Name _____

Festival and celebration stories

Celebration stories

Celebration stories

✤ Two celebration stories have been mixed up. Cut out the strips and put them in the right order to tell the story.

When it was dark, Katie put on her warm boots and thick coat.	Then Katie and her dad walked down to the local park.
He was excited because his brother was getting married.	'Stop daydreaming,' his mother called up the stairs. 'We're going to be late.'
As she watched, sparkling fireworks shot into the air.	Oliver put on his best silk shirt and admired himself proudly in the mirror.
Katie could see crowds of people around a huge bonfire.	He thought about the celebration party and all the delicious food.

✤ Write what you think will happen next in each story.

Teacher Timesavers: Story writing

91

Festival and celebration stories

Name _____

Festivals and events

Festivals and events

✤ Draw a line to match each event to the right picture.

Birthday    New Year    Easter

Divali

Event

- Parties are held at midnight

- A person receives presents

- Candles are lit in homes

- People give chocolate eggs

✤ Write the names of two other festivals or events. Then write about one thing that happens during each festival or event.

Teacher Timesavers: Story writing

Name _____

Festival and celebration stories

Santa's midnight journey

Santa's midnight journey

✤ List two action words for each sentence. One has been done for you.

Ideas: shone, sparkled, rang, whistled

- The wind ___swirled___ around the shiny sleigh.
  _____

- The stars _____ in the cold night sky.
  _____

  - The sleigh _____ through the sparkling snow.
    _____

  - Sleigh-bells _____ through the frosty air.
    _____

✤ Write a description of Santa's midnight journey.
Try to include the sentences you have already completed.

Teacher Timesavers: Story writing

93

Festival and celebration stories

Name _____

Describing festivals

Describing festivals

❖ Choose one festival you celebrate.

Festival _____ Date of festival _____

Reason why the festival is celebrated _____

❖ List the smells, sounds, colours and feelings you associate with the festival.

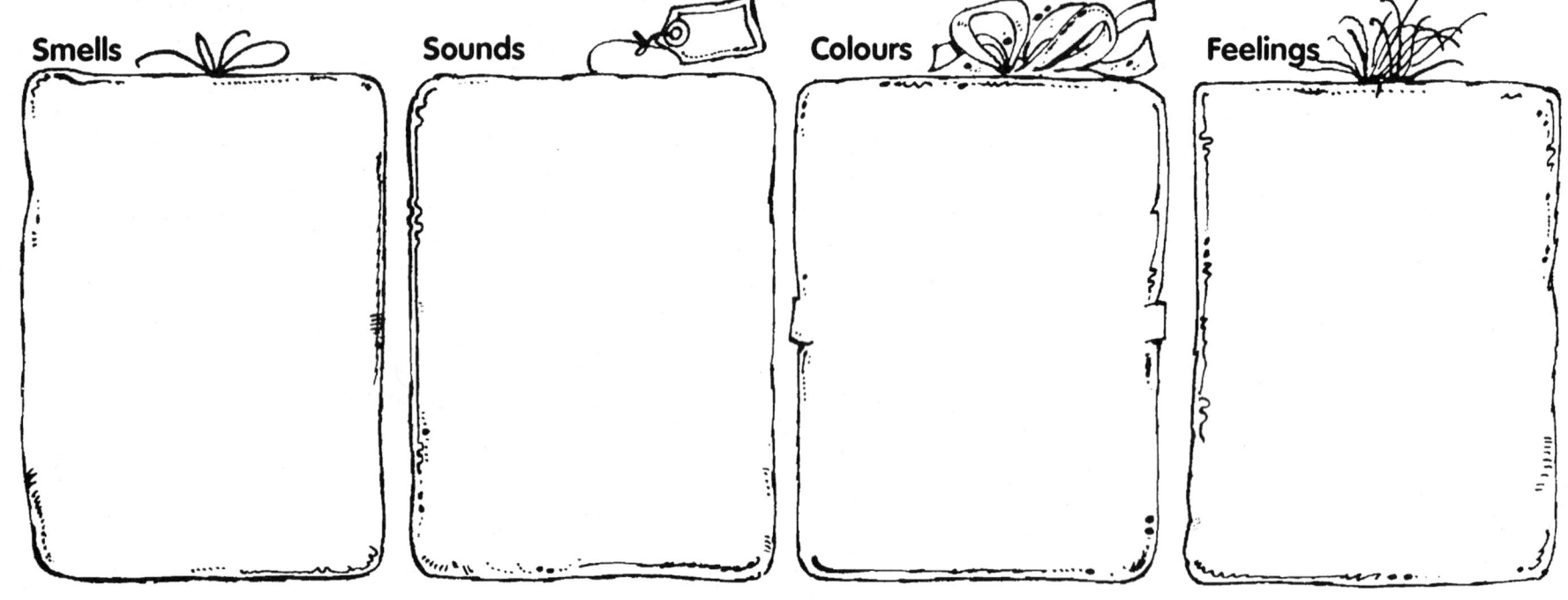

Smells	Sounds	Colours	Feelings

❖ Write a festival story to tell someone who has never celebrated it all about when it happens, why and the smells, sounds, colours and events.

Name _____

Festival and celebration stories

Festival titles

Festival titles

✤ List ideas for the festival, name of the main character and setting for these story titles.

Zahid's New Slippers

Festival

Setting

Character

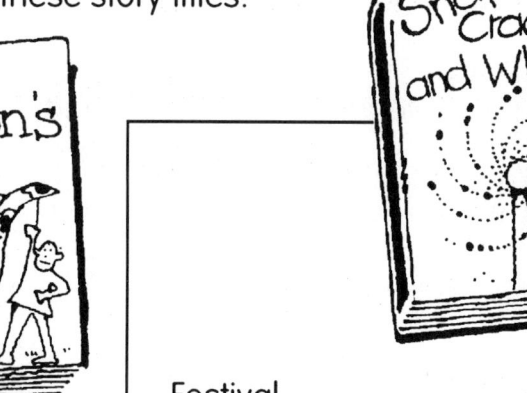

The Dragon's Tail

Festival

Setting

Character

Snap, Crackle and Whizz

Festival

Setting

Character

✤ Choose one title and write a story using the ideas you have listed.

Teacher Timesavers: Story writing

95

Festival and celebration stories

Name _____

Party story

Party story

♣ What kind of party would you like to write a story about?

☐ wedding   ☐ birthday   ☐ christening   ☐ other _____

♣ Plan the information about the party on the invitation and make a guest list of characters.

Party invitation

To _____
Please come to a _____ party
on _____
starting at _____
finishing at _____
place _____
from _____

Please reply

Guest list

_____
_____
_____
_____
_____
_____
_____
_____

♣ Write a story about the party.
Describe the guests, events, food and decorations.

Name _____

Historical stories

May's photographs

May's photographs

✤ Cut out these pictures of May. Put them in order to tell the story of May's life.

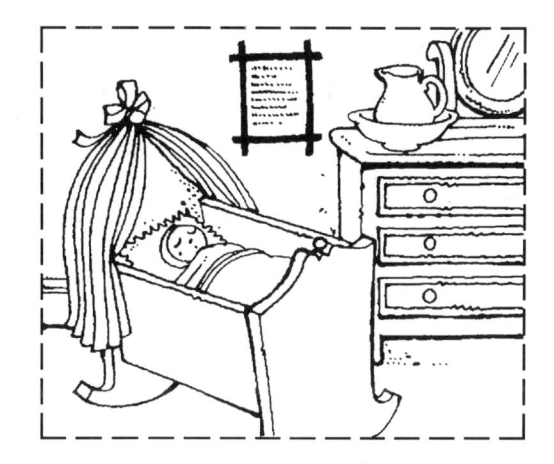

✤ Stick the pictures on a large sheet of paper and underneath each one write where May is and what she is doing.

Teacher Timesavers: Story writing

97

Historical stories

Albert's story

Albert's story

✤ Look at these things from Albert's bedroom which give you clues about Albert and his life. Plan some ideas for writing a story about Albert by answering these questions.

- What did Albert like to do in his spare time?

- What sort of clothes did Albert wear to school?

- Who did Albert live with?

- How old was Albert?

- When do you think Albert lived?

Teacher Timesavers: Story writing

Name _____

Historical stories

Time-travellers in Ancient Greece

Time-travellers in Ancient Greece

✤ Gaby and Nassar are time-travellers. Plan your ideas for a story about what happens to them when their time machine lands in Ancient Greece.

What sort of buildings will they see?

What food and drink will they have?

What sort of people will they meet?

Which gods and goddesses will they learn about?

To write your story continue this story opening.

The time dial on Gaby and Nassar's machine said 500BC. The place reading said Ancient Greece.
   Gaby slowly opened the door as the machine stopped shuddering. They stepped outside...

Teacher Timesavers: Story writing

99

Historical stories

Spanish Armada report

Spanish Armada report

Imagine you are an English sailor who watched the burning English galleons sail towards the Spanish Armada on 21 July 1588 at Calais.

✤ Write a description of what happened, in the form of a report, to send to Queen Elizabeth I.

Plan your ideas first. List words to describe:

how the Spanish galleons looked	what happened
how you felt	Other information
the colours, sounds and smells of the burning English galleons	

Start your report:

Your Royal Majesty, Queen Elizabeth

100

Teacher Timesavers: Story writing

Name _____

Historical stories

Railway journey

Railway journey

✤ Write a story describing a Victorian character's railway journey. Plan your ideas in each railway carriage.

| Beginning of story | Middle of story | End of story |

To help you

Trains were called steam locomotives

Locomotives travelled at 30 miles/50km per hour

Routes included
MANCHESTER – LIVERPOOL
GLASGOW – INVERNESS

Teacher Timesavers: Story writing

Historical stories

World War II diary

World War II diary

Name _____

✤ Which person will you write your diary as? (tick)

- [ ] a soldier
- [ ] a nurse
- [ ] your idea _____
- [ ] a child in a city
- [ ] an evacuee

Date

102

Teacher Timesavers: Story writing

Name _____

Historical stories
Time capsule

Time capsule

Imagine that you are a child living in the time you are learning about. Plan a time capsule which will tell people in the future all about your life.

♣ Describe or draw three everyday objects for the time capsule and say why you would include them.

because	because	because

♣ On the back of this sheet, write a letter to put in the time capsule. The letter should tell the reader about you and your life.

To whoever may find this time capsule,

My name is _____ . I was born on _____

In my family there are _____

Ideas

clothes
food
religion
school
entertainment
transport

Teacher Timesavers: Story writing

Historical stories

Historical settings

Name _____

Historical settings

✤ List words which describe an imaginary town or village during the period you are learning about.

- Buildings
- Sounds
- Transport
- Colours
- Name of town or village
- Jobs
- Other information
- Smells
- Appearance of poor people
- Appearance of rich people

✤ Write a description of your imaginary town or village. Use the words you have listed.

Teacher Timesavers: Story writing

Name _____

Mixed bag of stories

Weather story

Weather story

✤ Choose one of these titles and write a weather story.

Rain Rain Rain

Disaster as wind causes chaos

Heat wave

Motorway madness - fog causes smash

Snow blizzards sweep Britain

✤ Use coloured pencils to shade the words which describe the weather in your headline. List some words of your own.

pelting	lashing	swirling
dry	burning	falling
scorching	hot	whirling
floating	freezing	wet
_____	_____	_____
_____	_____	_____
_____	_____	_____

✤ Describe what effects your weather might have on:

the environment

people

animals

Teacher Timesavers: Story writing

105

Mixed bag of stories

Name _____

Weather myth

Weather myth

A myth is a traditional story. It usually includes imaginary characters or creatures. Myths are sometimes used to explain natural events.

♣ Plan ideas for a myth which could be used to explain each of the following types of weather.

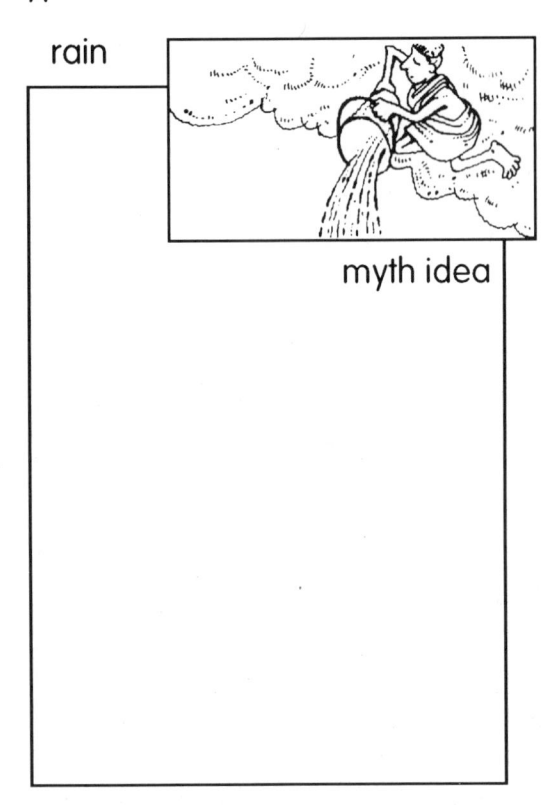

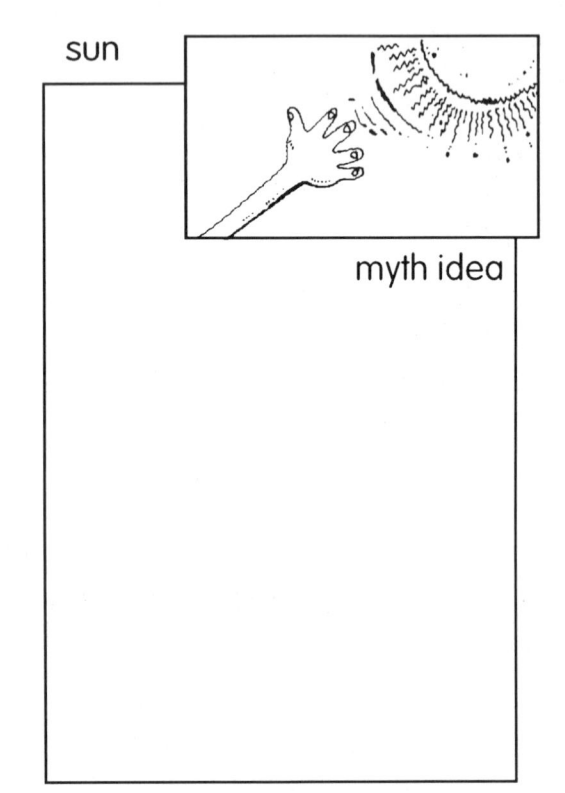

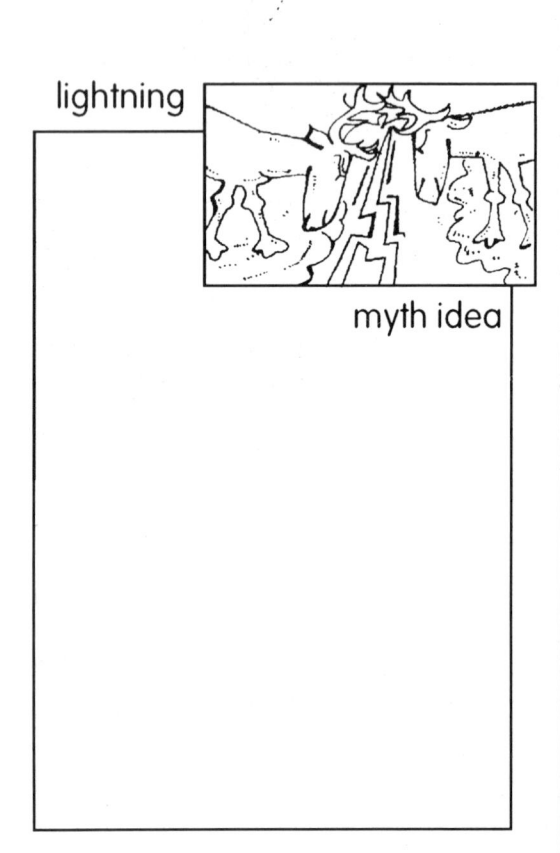

rain

myth idea

sun

myth idea

lightning

myth idea

♣ Write a weather myth.
Use one of the ideas you have outlined above or an idea of your choice.

Name _____

Mixed bag of stories

Secret places

Secret places

♣ Choose one of the following secret places as the setting for a story.

| A secret garden |
| A room in the attic |
| A hidden room |
| Your own idea |

♣ Plan your story by answering these questions.

How will your character discover the secret place?

Why has the place been kept secret?

How will your character feel when he or she discovers the secret place?

What will your character find there?

♣ Write a story about a secret place. Include a description of the place – its smells, colours and sounds.

Teacher Timesavers: Story writing

107

Mixed bag of stories

Name _____

Fire!

Fire!

✤ Draw a picture in the empty box to complete the story.

✤ Write the story shown in the pictures.
Give your story a title.

Teacher Timesavers: Story writing

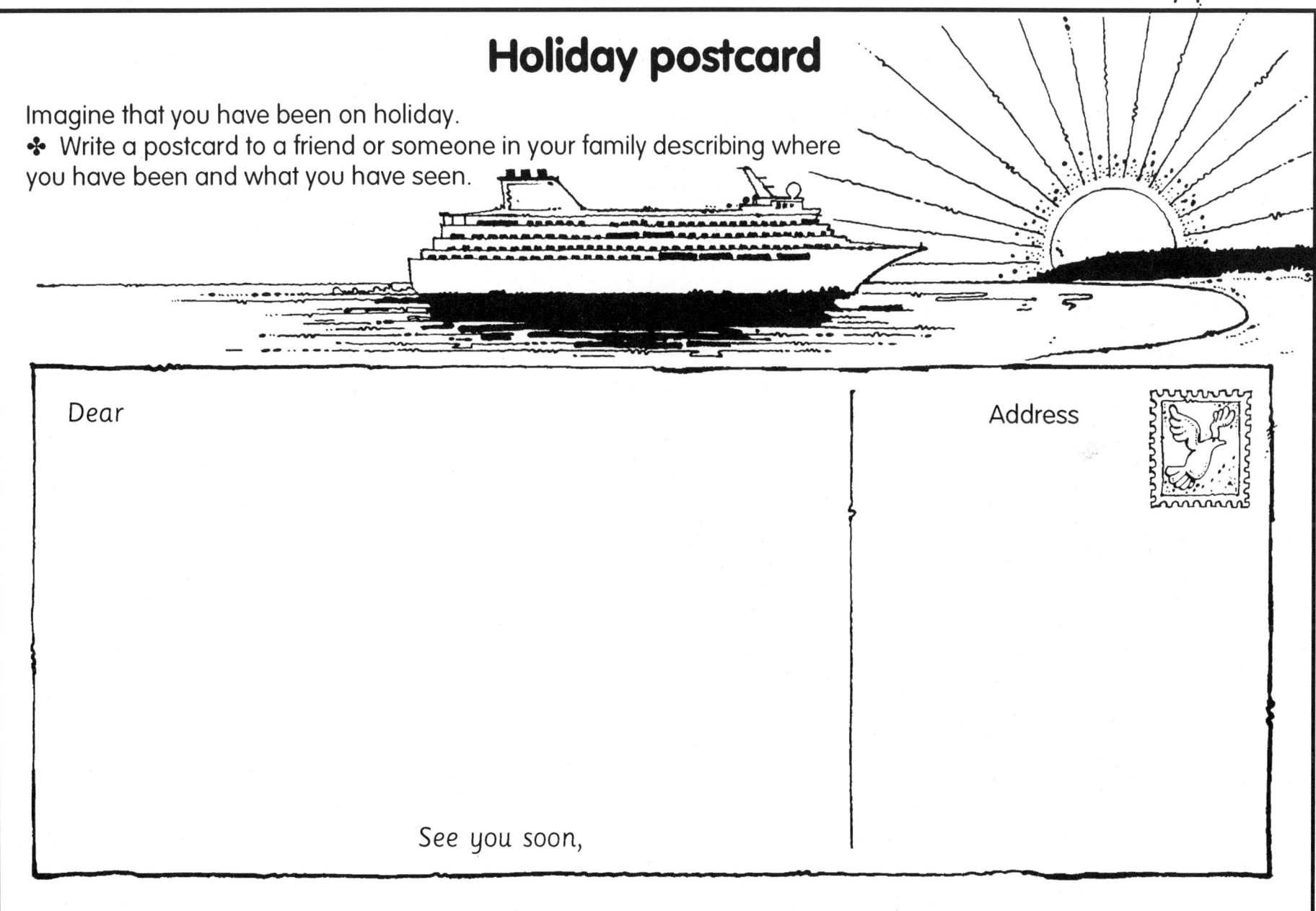

Name _____

Mixed bag of stories

Holiday postcard

Holiday postcard

Imagine that you have been on holiday.
♣ Write a postcard to a friend or someone in your family describing where you have been and what you have seen.

Dear

Address

See you soon,

Teacher Timesavers: Story writing

109

Mixed bag of stories

Name _____

Into the future

Into the future

Plan a story where your main character travels into the future.

♣ Tick how your character will travel:

☐ a time machine ☐ through a secret door ☐ while asleep ☐ your own idea _____

♣ What year will your character travel to? ☐

♣ What will your character find different in the future?

Ideas

countryside
buildings
architecture
fashion
music
food
school
entertainment

♣ Now write your own story.

110

Teacher Timesavers: Story writing

Name _____

Mixed bag of stories

Western story

Western story

✤ List each of the ingredients under the correct heading below. Add some more ingredients ideas of your own.

Characters	Objects	Places	Events

✤ Write a Western story opening. Describe either a character, place, object or event.

Ingredients

cowboy hat	bar/saloon
horses	rescuing someone
chase	jailhouse
stagecoach	ranch
sheriff	wanted poster
dusty plain	leather boots
cowboy	barmaid
fights	hiding from the law

Teacher Timesavers: Story writing

111

Mixed bag of stories

Science story

Name _____

Science story

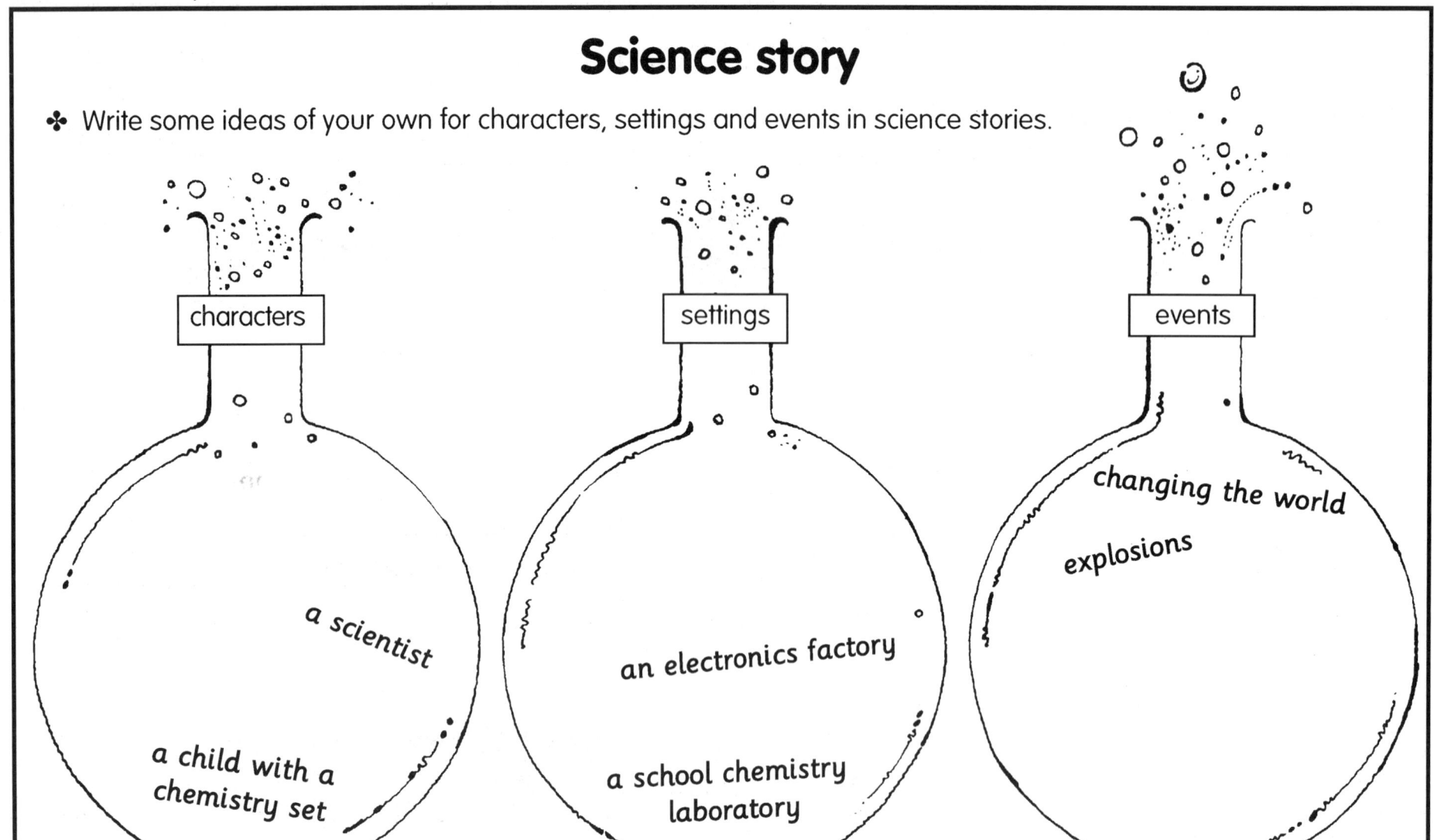

✤ Write some ideas of your own for characters, settings and events in science stories.

characters
- a scientist
- a child with a chemistry set

settings
- an electronics factory
- a school chemistry laboratory

events
- changing the world
- explosions

✤ Choose at least one ingredient from each bottle.
Mix the ingredients together in a story.

Name _____

Mixed bag of stories

Shipwreck

Shipwreck

Imagine that you are walking along a cliff-top and you see a shipwreck.
♣ Write a description of the shipwreck happening on the rocks below you.

As I was walking along the cliff-top it started to rain. I looked out to sea and saw

Describe:

- the ship
- the sea
- the sky and weather
- what happens

Use:

swirling
gushing
heaving
crashing
racing

Teacher Timesavers: Story writing

Mixed bag of stories

Name _____

Musical story

Musical story

✤ Choose one of the following instruments.

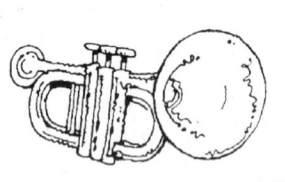

other _____

✤ Complete the factfile below about the instrument you chose.

Instrument factfile

The instrument plays (tick)

☐ high notes   ☐ low notes   ☐ loudly   ☐ softly

Which family of instruments does it belong to? (tick)

☐ brass   ☐ woodwind   ☐ string   ☐ other

How would someone play the instrument? (tick)

☐ blow it   ☐ strike it   ☐ pluck it   ☐ other

✤ Write a story about the instrument you chose.

Ideas

• A young child is given the instrument as a present.

• The instrument is found in a garage by a family when they move into their new home.

• A child who wants to win a local music competition sees the instrument in a shop window.

• Your own idea.

114

Teacher Timesavers: Story writing

Name _____

Mixed bag of stories

Aircraft story

Aircraft story

Imagine that you are the passesnger in an aeroplane when the pilot collapses.
♣ Write the dialogue between you and the airport control tower.

ME	Help, the pilot has collapsed!
AIRPORT	Don't panic! What is your altitude?
ME	Um, 12 000 metres, I think.
AIRPORT	

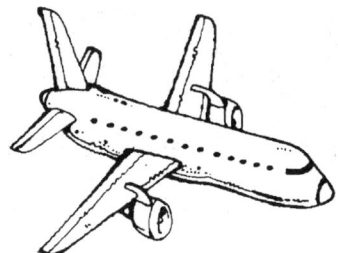

Aircraft language

altitude –
how high up you are

rudder –
needed to steer

wing flap –
needed to land

control tower

runway

throttle – makes the plane go faster and slower

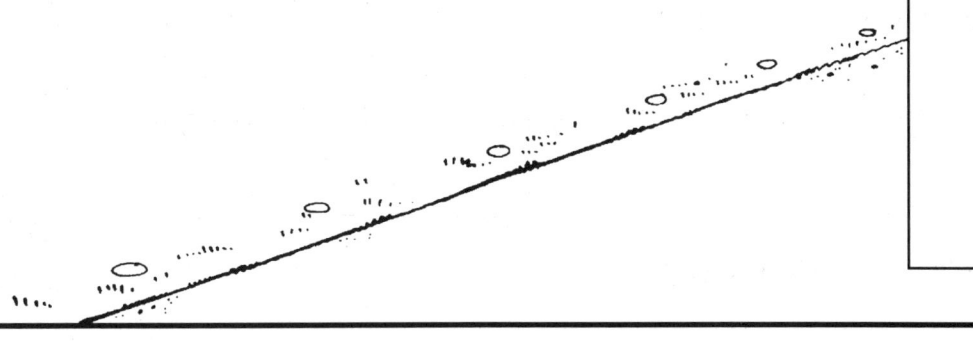

Teacher Timesavers: Story writing

Mixed bag of stories

The incredible present

Name _____

The incredible present

♣ Continue the following story opening.

Eve was looking out of her bedroom window. She could see her aunt walking up the drive towards the house. In her arms Aunt Zara was carrying a box, wrapped in brightly coloured paper.

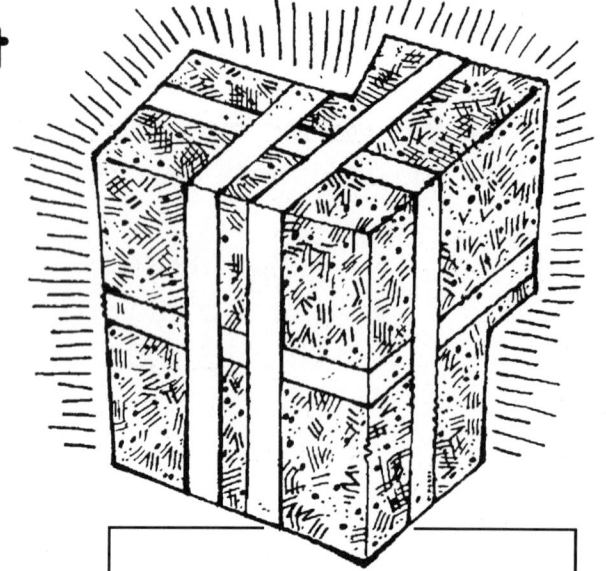

Ideas

Who will the present be for?

What will be in the box?

How will the character feel when he or she opens the present?

Why will the present be incredible?

Name _____

Mixed bag of stories

Changing places

Changing places

✤ Choose a person you know well.

✤ Write a diary extract as if you are that person describing your day.

parent   friend   teacher   your idea

Today I didn't wake up until 8 o'clock. Disaster! I knew I would be very late and I felt

Describe:

- what the person does
- where they go
- who they meet
- how they feel
- what they think about

Teacher Timesavers: Story writing

117

Mixed bag of stories

Name _____

Pollution

Pollution

✤ Complete this chart. Use the last column for your own ideas.

Type of pollution	car fumes	litter	oil spills	cigarettes	
What causes it?					
What are its effects?					
Who can clean it?					
How can it be cleaned?					

✤ Choose one form of pollution and write a story about it.
Try to use adjectives to describe the pollution and its effects.

Teacher Timesavers: Story writing

Name _____

Mixed bag of stories

How do they feel?

How do they feel?

♣ Write down words which describe how each character is feeling. Explain why the character feels this way.

He feels

because

She feels

because

He feels

because

She feels

because

Teacher Timesavers: Story writing

119

Mixed bag of stories

Competition story

Name _____

Competition story

✤ Choose one of the following competitions (tick).

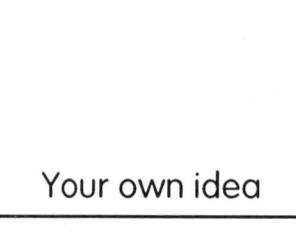

| ☐ Pet show | ☐ TV quiz | ☐ Crossword | ☐ Your own idea |

✤ Write a story about the competition you chose.
Try to make your story as exciting, tense and action-packed as possible.
Plan your ideas first below.

- Character(s)

- Setting

- Name of competition

- What will happen

- How the story will end

Teacher Timesavers: Story writing

Name _____

Mixed bag of stories
Cautionary tales

Cautionary tales

> Cautionary tales are stories which show what happens to imaginary people or animals when they behave badly or do something wrong.

♣ Suggest some ideas for cautionary tales by listing possible bad behaviour or actions, the consequences of these actions, and the characters and setting for each one.

	Idea 1	Idea 2	Idea 3
Bad behaviour/actions	Being mean	Arguing all the time	
Consequences	People aren't generous to you		
Characters			
Setting			

Teacher Timesavers: Story writing

Mixed bag of stories

Disaster!

Name _____

Disaster!

✤ Plan the ingredients for these disaster stories.

Disaster	Setting	Effects
fire 		
earthquake 		
avalanche 		
tidal wave 		

✤ Write a story which shows the effects of one of these disasters on the setting you have chosen.

Name _____

Mixed bag of stories

Story titles: 1

Story titles: 1

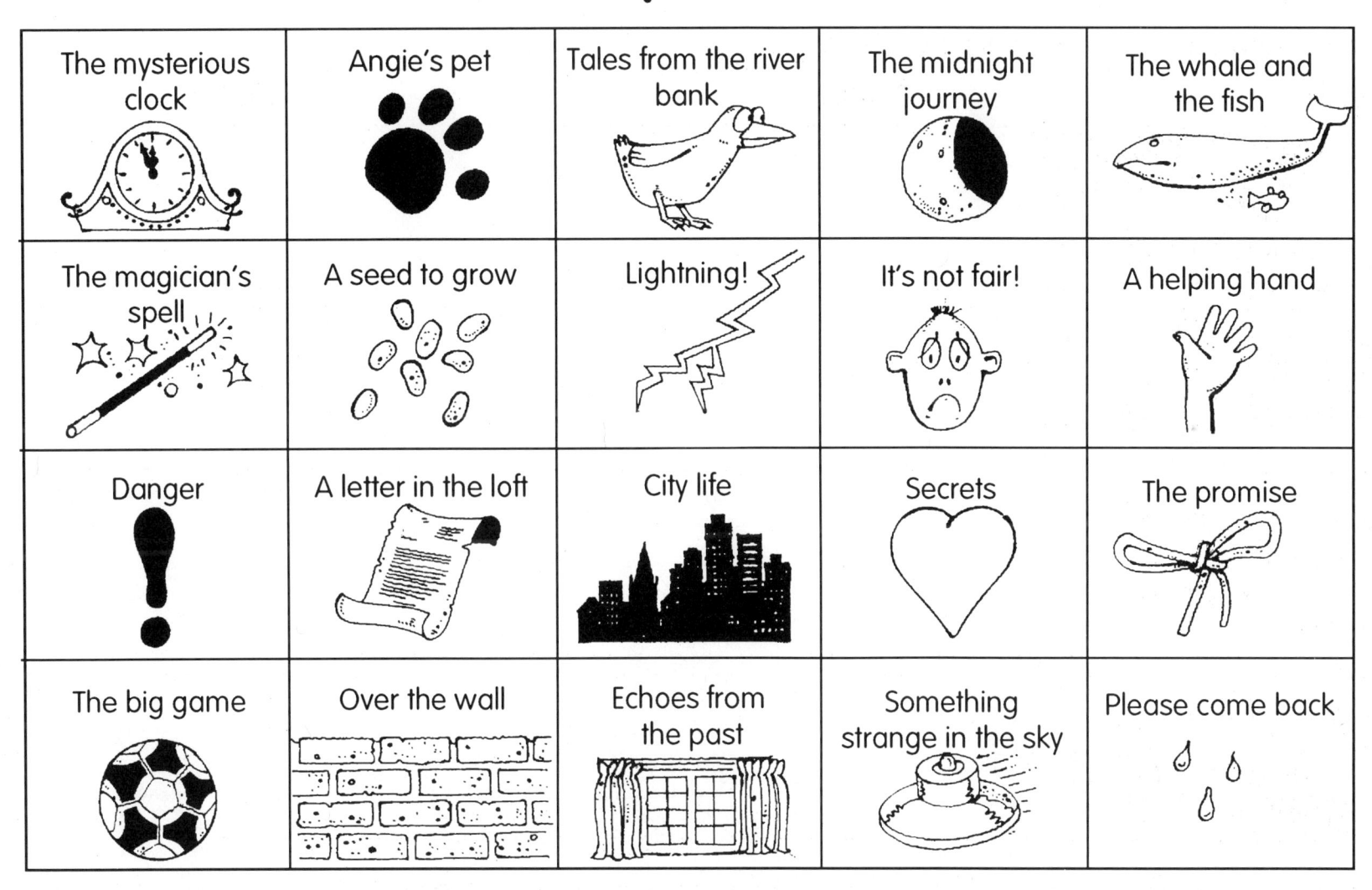

The mysterious clock	Angie's pet	Tales from the river bank	The midnight journey	The whale and the fish
The magician's spell	A seed to grow	Lightning!	It's not fair!	A helping hand
Danger	A letter in the loft	City life	Secrets	The promise
The big game	Over the wall	Echoes from the past	Something strange in the sky	Please come back

✤ Write a story using one of these titles.

Teacher Timesavers: Story writing

123

Mixed bag of stories

Name _____

Story titles: 2

Story titles: 2

♣ Write two possible story titles beside each picture.

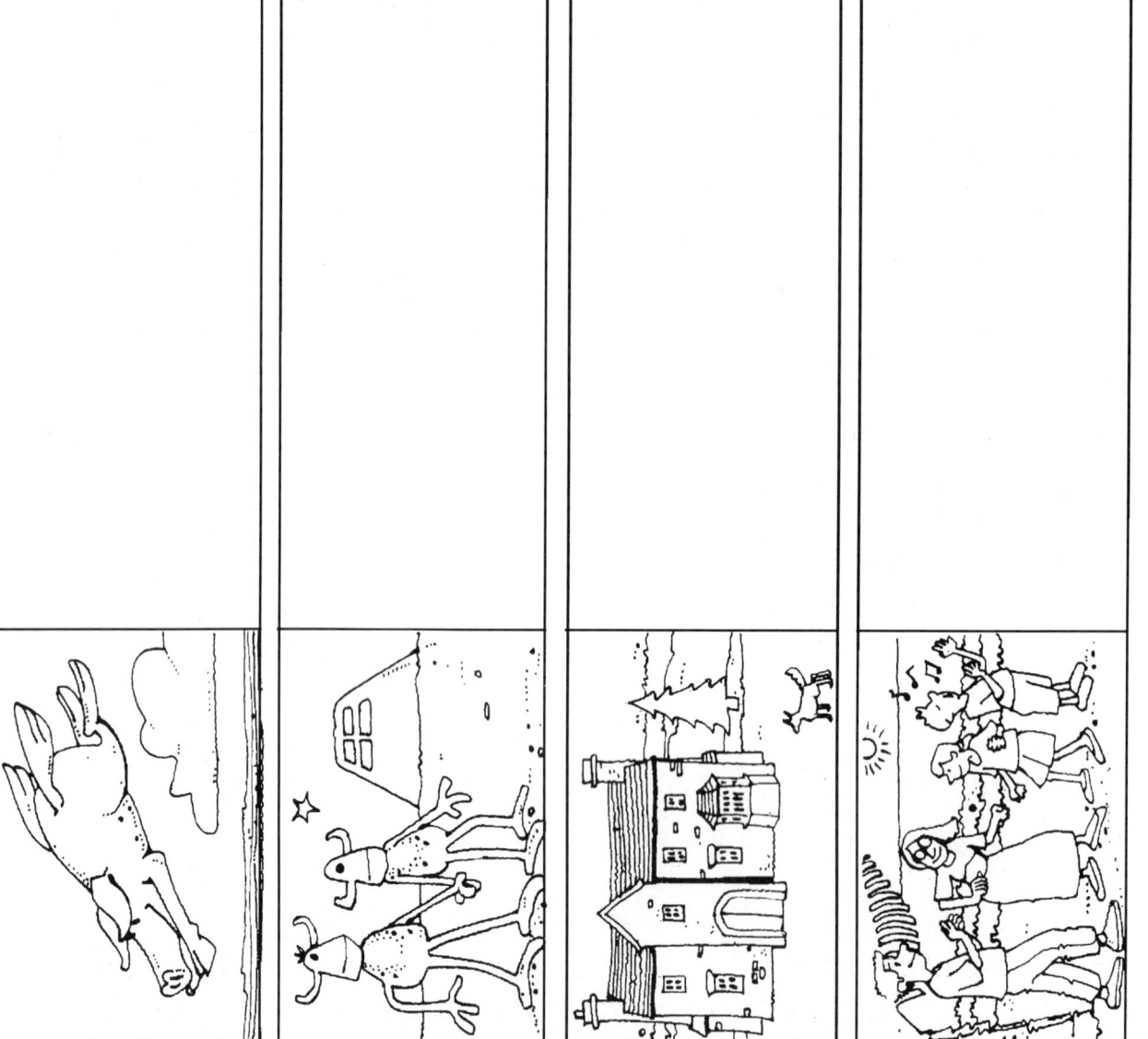

♣ Write a story with one of the titles you have listed.

124   Teacher Timesavers: Story writing

Name _____

Redrafting and language skills
Redrafting your story

Redrafting your story

♣ Have you: (tick)

- checked that each sentence starts with a capital letter and ends with a full stop? ☐

- checked your spelling? ☐

- started a new paragraph each time the place, event or time changes? ☐

- used speech marks around the words characters say and started a new line every time a character talks? ☐

- read your story aloud to check that you've written what you meant to? ☐

- made your story interesting to read by:

  – writing a good opening? ☐

  – describing the setting? ☐

  – writing a good ending? ☐

  – describing the characters? ☐

- thought about the best words to use? ☐

♣ On the back of this sheet write what you are pleased with about your story. Is there anything about your story you would like to change to make it better?

Redrafting and language skills

Name _____

Choosing the best words

Choosing the best words

When you write a story you can choose which words you think are best.

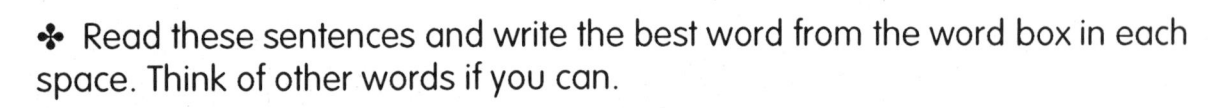

✤ Read these sentences and write the best word from the word box in each space. Think of other words if you can.

- When Harriet saw the bat she felt _____.

    | scared |
    | horrified |
    | afraid |
    | sick |
    | terrified |

- The music on the waltzer was _____.

    | loud |
    | noisy |
    | deafening |
    | blasting |

- The _____ lake shimmered before them.

    | big |
    | huge |
    | enormous |
    | sparkling |

- After Aziz stumped his toe all he was able to do was to _____.

    | hobble |
    | limp |
    | shuffle |
    | stagger |
    | totter |

Think carefully about the words you choose in your story.

To help you — use a thesaurus

126

Teacher Timesavers: Story writing

Name _____

Redrafting and language skills

The language of story writing

The language of story writing

The following words are used to describe stories:
plot – storyline
events – things that happen in the story
setting – places in the story
characters – people in the story
title – story name
author – story writer

✤ List the information about the story on the book jacket under the right heading below.

Book jacket text:
- Red Riding Hood returns to try and save her aunty from the wicked wolf.
- Red Riding Hood visits her aunty
- Aunty and Red Riding Hood take a walk in the wood
- The wicked wolf sneaks into Aunty's house

Red Riding Hood II
By Roger Sajit
SCHOLASTIC

plot storyline

events things that happen

setting places

characters people

title story name

author writer

Teacher Timesavers: Story writing

127

Redrafting and language skills
Writing in sentences

Name _____

Writing in sentences

In your writing each sentence must start with a capital letter and end with a full stop.

✤ Read the description. Decide where you think there should be full stops.
After each full stop put a capital letter. The first sentence has been done for you.

A cool breeze blew across the beach. tiny grains of dry sand danced in the air the waves lapped lazily on to the beach white bubbles frothed at the water's edge and then vanished like magic into the sand

slowly the sun rose over the bay seagulls began to call urgently from the cliffs small mites started to burrow and scurry in the shaded rock pools below another day had begun.

Teacher Timesavers: Story writing

Name _____

Redrafting and language skills

Bag of nouns

Bag of nouns

Nouns are words that name people, places, objects or ideas.

♣ Sort the bag of nouns below into the right lists.

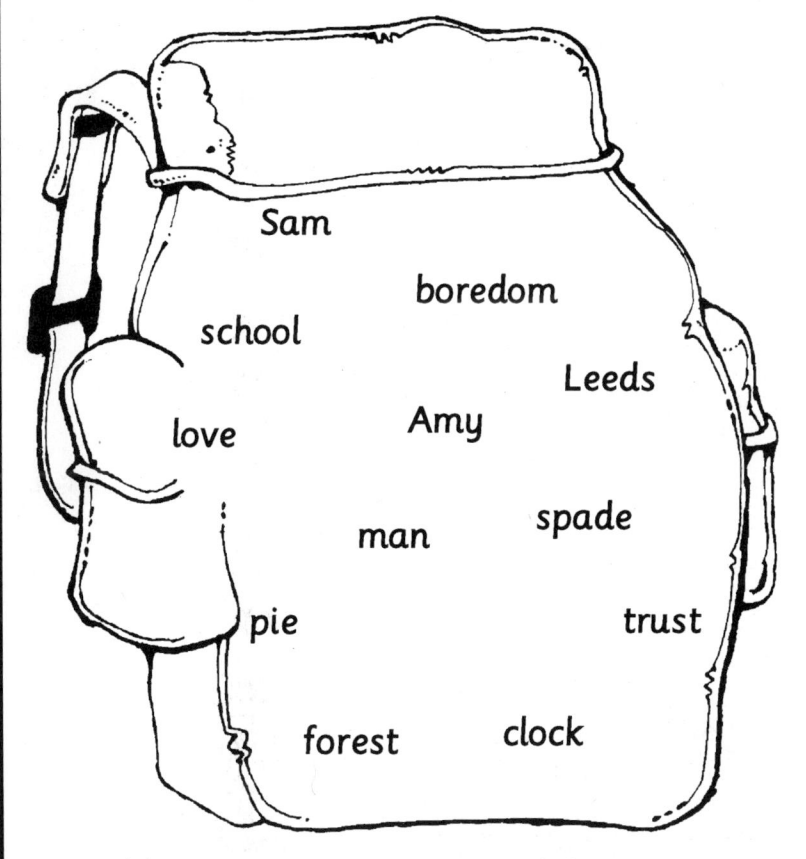

Words in the bag: Sam, boredom, school, Leeds, love, Amy, man, spade, pie, trust, forest, clock

people	places
Sam	

objects	ideas

♣ Add some more nouns to each list.

Teacher Timesavers: Story writing

129

Redrafting and language skills

Name _____

All sorts of nouns

All sorts of nouns

There are different sorts of nouns.

> **proper noun** – starts with a capital letter and names a person or place
> **common noun** – names an object or thing
> **abstract noun** – names a thing that cannot be seen, touched, tasted, heard or smelled
> **collective noun** – names a group or collection of things
> **single noun** – names a single person or thing
> **plural noun** – names more than one person or thing

♣ Choose a different colour for each sort of noun and colour the boxes.
Shade each of the words with a colour to show what sort of noun it is.

Everest
book
London
swarm
Meg
sandwich
Manchester United
cameras
anger
peace
child
pencil

☐ proper
☐ common
☐ abstract
☐ collective
☐ single
☐ plural

130

Teacher Timesavers: Story writing

Name _____

Redrafting and language skills

Adjectives

Adjectives

Adjectives are words that tell us more about nouns – people, places, objects or ideas.

♣ Write an adjective below each picture.

adjectives

happy
naughty
four
tasty

_____ person   _____ books   _____ dog 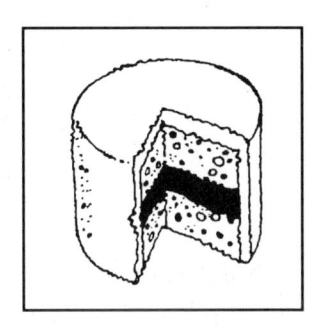   _____ cake

♣ Draw a picture in each box.

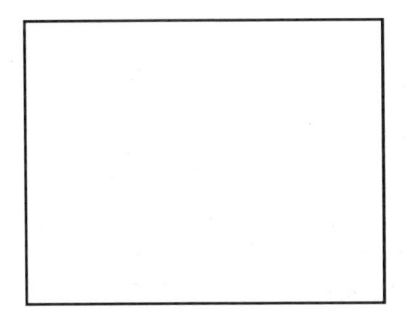

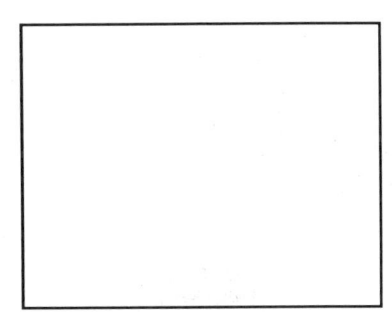

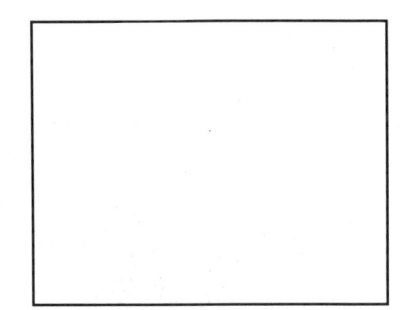

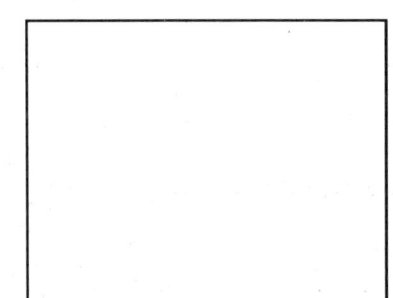

_____ cat   _____ forest   _____ jumper   _____ bag

♣ Write an adjective which describes the object you have drawn.

Teacher Timesavers: Story writing

131

Redrafting and language skills
Verbs

Name _____

Verbs

A verb is a word which shows what a person or object is doing.
A verb is an *action* word.

✤ Match each verb in the verb box with the right picture.

verb box

jump
run
catch
think

✤ List verbs which describe the action of the person or thing in each picture.

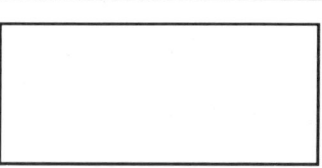

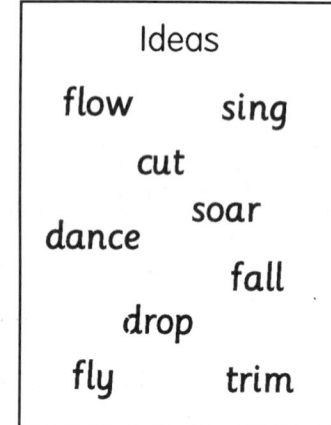

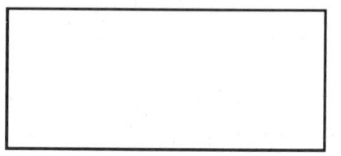

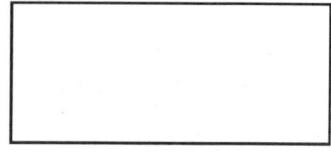

Ideas

flow   sing
   cut
        soar
dance
        fall
   drop
fly   trim

132

Teacher Timesavers: Story writing

Name _____

Redrafting and language skills

Adverbs

Adverbs

Adverbs explain how, when or where the action happens.

✤ Underline the adverbs in each sentence.

How	I walked slowly to school.	The pie cooked quickly.	
When	I went to the dentist today.	Yesterday Mum cleaned the car.	
Where	I saw Jamie there.	We walked towards the house.	

✤ In the third set of boxes write your own sentences, using an adverb to explain how, when or where the action happened.

Teacher Timesavers: Story writing

133

Redrafting and language skills

Conjunctions

Conjunctions

A conjunction is a joining word.

and   as   but   although   so   because

♣ Underline the conjunctions in this story opening:

It was a cold day and snow lay on the ground. Birds shivered in their nests because a chilling wind blew through the trees. Daylight arrived slowly as the sun rose lazily. There was no sign of human life although trails of smoke rose from many of the chimney pots.

♣ Add conjunctions to this story opening:

The pupils in Class 4 were all working very hard _____ they did not notice the spaceship land. At first no one was aware of it _____ the metal dome came to rest just outside the classroom window. Suddenly, all 24 pairs of eyes looked up in unison _____ there was a deafening noise. The door of the spaceship opened slowly _____ three purple aliens appeared.

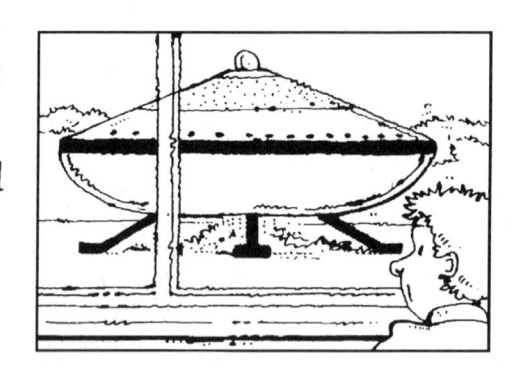

♣ Choose one of the story openings above and rewrite it on a separate sheet. Miss out each conjunction and put a full stop in its place. Start the next word with a capital letter. Then read the story opening with and without the conjunctions. Write down which you think works best and say why.

Teacher Timesavers: Story writing

Name _____

Redrafting and language skills
Paragraphs

Paragraphs

Paragraphs help you to organise your writing into sections.

♣ Decide how to organise this story opening into sections. Put // when:

- the story starts
- the time changes
- the place changes

♣ Continue the story, using paragraphs to organise your writing.
To show you are starting a new paragraph:

- start a new line
- indent your writing

It was the morning of the big game. James snuggled into the warmth of his duvet, thinking nervously about the day ahead of him. At 8 o'clock his alarm rang. He sighed. This meant he had to get up. He flung back the duvet and eased his feet into his slippers. Finally he made his way across the room. In the kitchen his dad was cooking breakfast. James knew his dad was only trying to help, but he felt too sick to eat. Across the street Ezzie was ready. As he put new laces in his boots he thought about winning the match. He was sure his team would win. He couldn't wait!

Teacher Timesavers: Story writing

Redrafting and language skills

Name _____

Direct speech

Direct speech

To help you
- Each time a character speaks start a new line.
- Put speech marks at the beginning and end of words characters say.

✤ Write the words each character is saying inside speech marks.

[Illustration: Father Bear saying "Who's been sitting in my chair?" and Baby Bear saying "And who's broken my chair?"]

Father Bear asked, '_____

_____?'

'_____

_____?' Baby Bear cried.

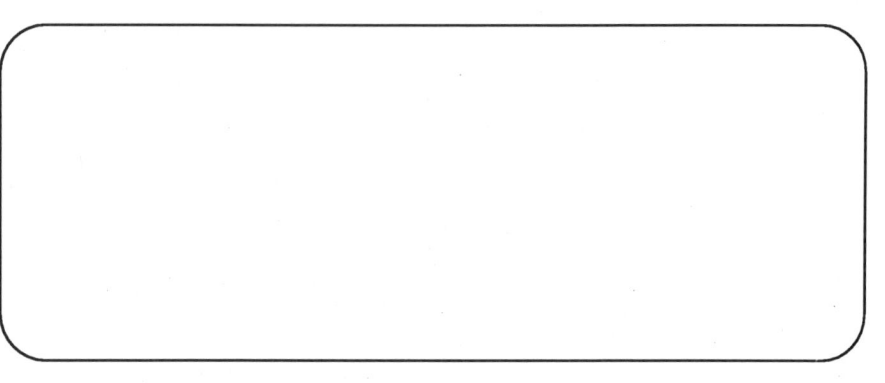

[Illustration: Cinderella saying "I'd like to go to the ball." and Fairy Godmother saying "Then you shall, Cinderella."]

✤ Write a conversation between two characters in a story you know well. Set the conversation out using direct speech.

136

Teacher Timesavers: Story writing

Name _____

Redrafting and language skills

Story tenses

Story tenses

✤ Read the story extracts below.

Decide whether each is written in the past tense, eg. *Andrew stepped on to the plane. He sat down.* or in the present tense, eg. *Andrew steps on to the plane. He sits down.*

✤ Underline the words that helped you decide.   ✤ Rewrite each extract using the opposite tense.

Using all of his strength Andrew leaped across the pit of snakes. He landed on the wet grass with a thud. Behind him the snakes hissed angrily.

| past | present |

He reaches across and picks up the diamond. His heart is racing. It seems, for a moment, as if the diamond is going to slip from his grasp.

| past | present |

Teacher Timesavers: Story writing

137

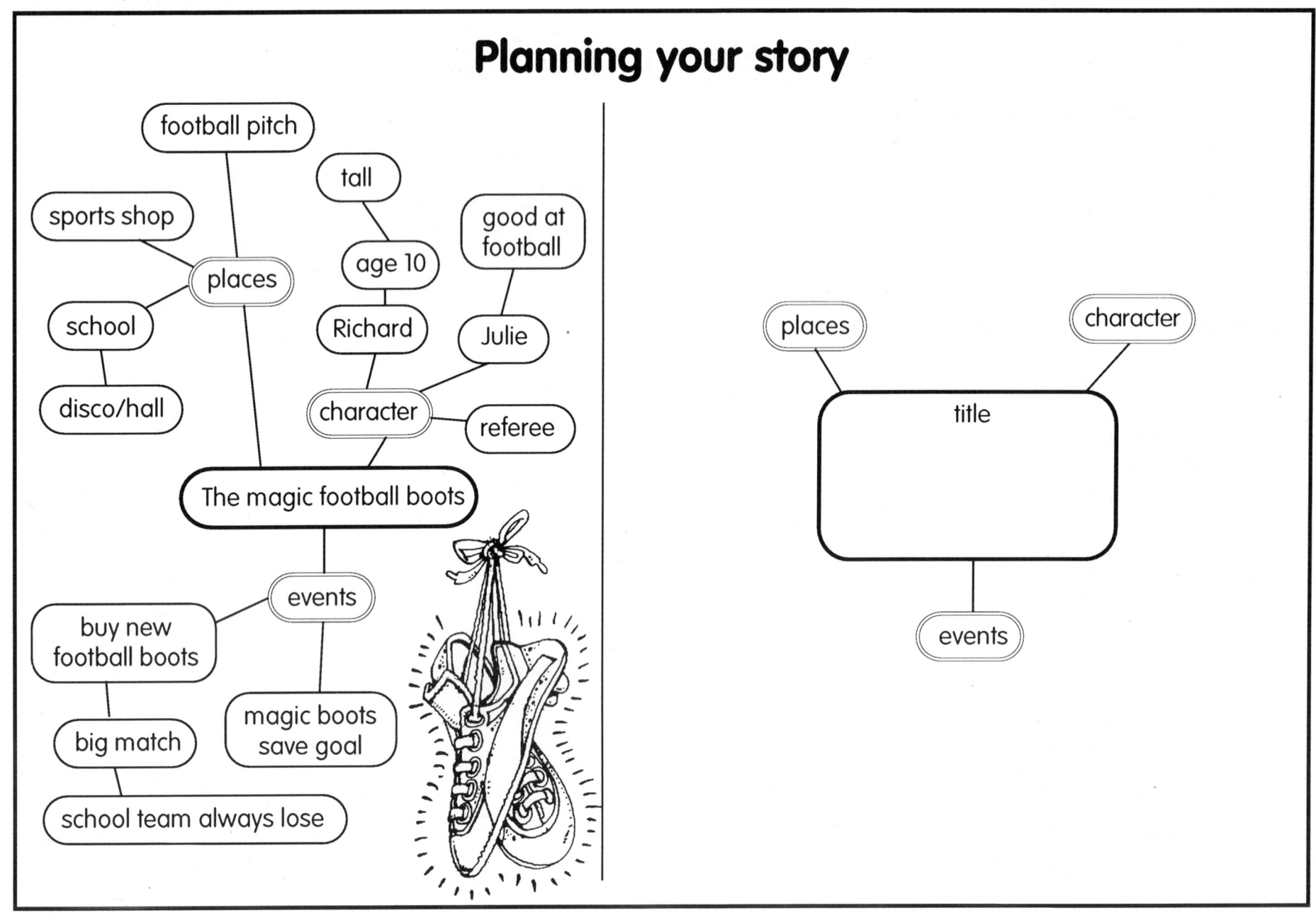

Pro formas
Planning your story

Name _____

Planning your story

Left mind map: "The magic football boots"

- places
  - football pitch
  - sports shop
  - school
  - disco/hall
- character
  - tall
  - age 10
  - Richard
  - good at football
  - Julie
  - referee
- events
  - buy new football boots
  - big match
  - school team always lose
  - magic boots save goal

Right mind map:
- title
  - places
  - character
  - events

138

Teacher Timesavers: Story writing

Name _____

Pro formas

Writing story openings

Writing story openings

♣ Write four different story openings.
Choose which one you like best for your story.

Describe the character.

Describe the place.

Describe what is happening.

Write what characters are saying.

Teacher Timesavers: Story writing

139

Pro formas

Name _____

Describing the character

Describing the character

♣ List words to describe your character.

eyes		nose
mouth	Drawing of my character	body type
hair	personality	clothes

140

Teacher Timesavers: Story writing

Name _____

Pro formas

Describing the setting

Describing the setting

✤ List words to describe your setting.

| sounds | | weather |

Drawing of my setting

| smells | | objects |

| | colours | |

Teacher Timesavers: Story writing

141

Pro formas
Storyboard

Name _____

Storyboard

✤ List or draw your ideas in these boxes.

1.	2.	3.
4.	5.	6.

Teacher Timesavers: Story writing

Name _____

Pro formas

Problems and solutions

Problems and solutions

♣ List your character's problems and how he or she will solve them.

problems

solutions

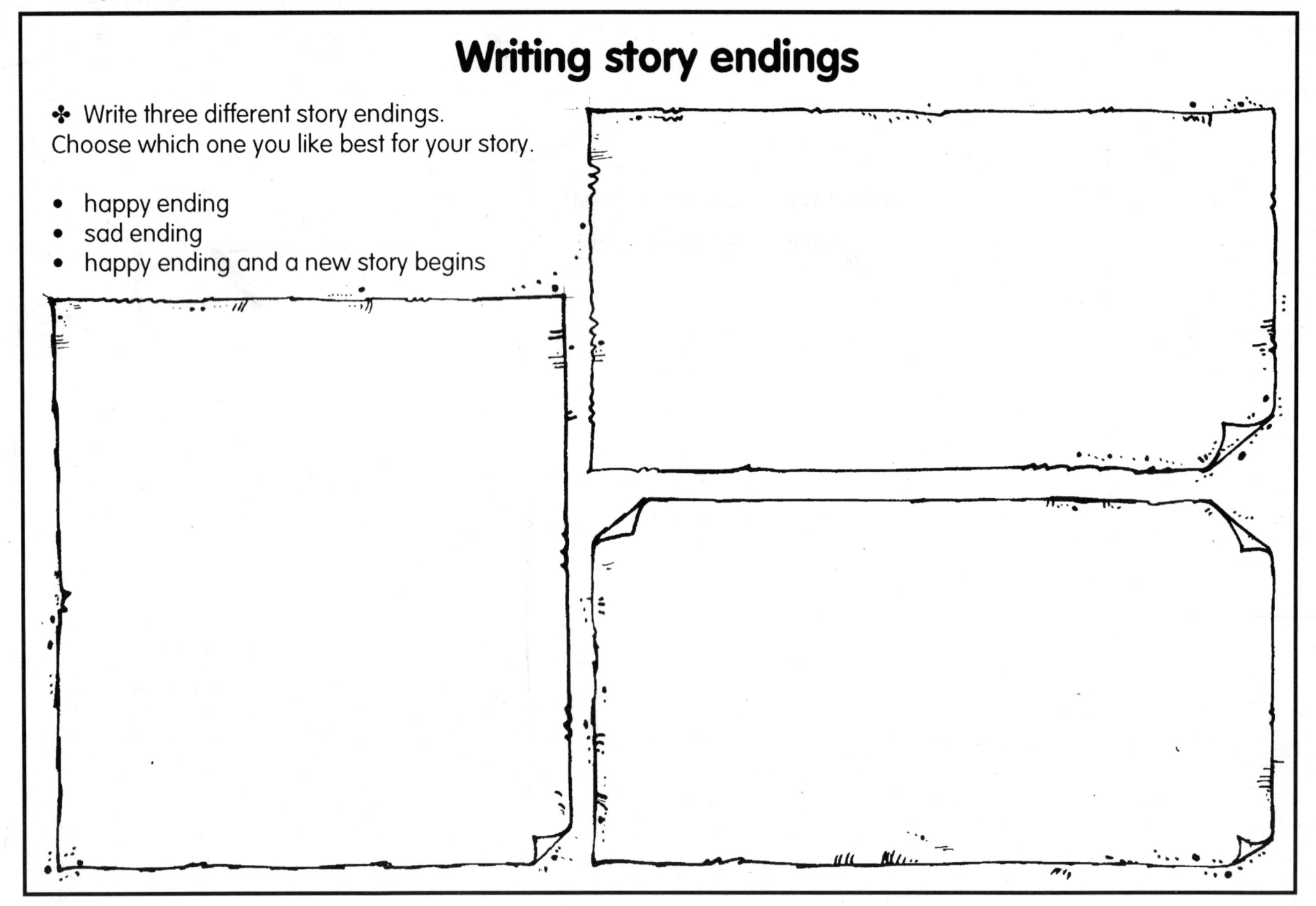

Pro formas
Writing story endings

Name _____

Writing story endings

♣ Write three different story endings.
Choose which one you like best for your story.

- happy ending
- sad ending
- happy ending and a new story begins